Awakened

by

AUTISM

Hay House Titles of Related Interest

Awakened
by
AUTISM

*Embracing Autism, Self, and
Hope for a New World*

Andrea Libutti, M.D.

HAY HOUSE, INC.
Carlsbad, California • New York City
London • Sydney • Johannesburg
Vancouver • Hong Kong • New Delhi

Published and distributed in the United States by: Hay House, Inc.: www.hayhouse
.com® • *Published and distributed in Australia by:* Hay House Australia Pty. Ltd.:
www.hayhouse.com.au • *Published and distributed in the United Kingdom by:* Hay
House UK, Ltd.: www.hayhouse.co.uk • *Published and distributed in the Republic
of South Africa by:* Hay House SA (Pty), Ltd.: www.hayhouse.co.za • *Distributed
in Canada by:* Raincoast Books: www.raincoast.com • *Published in India by:* Hay
House Publishers India: www.hayhouse.co.in

Project editor: Nicolette Salamanca Young • *Cover design:* Nita Ybarra
Interior design: Pamela Homan

Cataloging-in-Publication Data is on file with the Library of Congress

Tradepaper ISBN: 978-1-4019-4544-2

10 9 8 7 6 5 4 3 2 1
1st edition, April 2015

Printed in the United States of America

To my three beacons of light:
Jack, Sam, and Ben.
And to all children,
whose light will show us the way.

CONTENTS

INTRODUCTION

Recently, my three boys were playing in the playroom. I was in the kitchen, and as it had been a few minutes since I had heard any noise I went in to see what they were doing. Jack was sifting through a box of Lego pieces, and Sammy and Ben were playing with their Pokémon cards.

I knew that Jack was likely to want to incorporate other pieces into his play, so I went over to the bookshelf to take a box down that contained a different building set. But as I pulled the box off the shelf, I jostled a box of paint supplies.

"Ouch!" I said. "That really hurt!"

The box of paint supplies had hit me smack on the nose.

"Are you okay, Mommy?" Ben asked.

"Did you get hurt?" Sammy asked.

"I'm okay," I said. I felt a bit silly that I got clobbered that way.

Sammy and Ben resumed their play, but Jack put down the Lego that he had been examining. Then, he came over to me.

"Mommy got hurt," he said. He looked at me, and then he put his hands on my face.

"You need a kiss to feel better," he continued.

And with that, he kissed my face and smiled.

Of course, all parents enjoy when their children are particularly sweet and kind to others. In that moment, I was no exception. I loved how Jack had felt the need to come over to me and give me a kiss. It warmed my heart.

But it also made me stop and think. How could it be that Jack could show that level of empathy? That he behaved as he did was certainly a far cry from what I had been told would ever be possible for him.

You see, eight years prior to the moment when I got clobbered on the nose by the box of paint, Jack was diagnosed with severe autism. When that happened, I was told there was very little hope that Jack would ever be able to communicate with me or anyone else in any sort of meaningful way. I was told that he would rarely show empathy for others, and that significant relationships were out of the question.

I am so glad I didn't listen.

The Condition We Know as Autism

When you find out for the first time that a child in your life has autism, how do you feel? Do you feel exhilarated, like you just found out that he is a genius who is destined to become the President of the United States? Or do you feel devastated? Do you feel like the rug has been ripped out from under you? Do you feel that all of your hopes and dreams for the child have been dashed?

Like many other parents or caretakers, you may have felt deep disappointment, grief, frustration, and a level of pain that can be unbearable. I know; I was there. I remember feeling hopelessness and despair when Jack was first diagnosed. I remember the fear and uncertainty that constantly gnawed at me when I thought that he would never have any sort of meaningful relationships, and that he might not ever be able to respond to me when I spoke to him. I couldn't sleep, I couldn't eat, and I certainly couldn't see any glimmer of hope. I was devastated.

Autism is tough on parents for several reasons. Our children likely suffer from poor health in the form of digestive problems, chronic inflammation, and an impaired immune system. They have unusual and bizarre behaviors that we don't understand, which likely provoke awkward stares when we go out in public. But perhaps the hardest thing for us to cope with is our children's inability to connect with us. They don't look at us, talk to us, or laugh with us. They don't respond to us. It is like we don't exist to them.

We are told autism is a lifelong condition. We are told that perhaps our child will never talk, or if he does, there is no hope for anything of substance to be shared. We hear that there is not much that can be done other than some behavior therapy and medication to control aggressive behaviors. Or worse, we hear that someday we may have to institutionalize our child.

As an emergency room physician, I had direct access to many biomedical therapies. I knew where to look for the latest innovations, had conversations with a variety of medical professionals, and had a viable frame of reference for implementing plans of action. If a cure existed for the condition we know as autism, I was in a prime position to find it. My career also earned me access to practitioners who specialized in autism and helped inform my work when, after several years of a mentorship, I started a private practice to serve children with autism.

But the more I searched for a cure, the more disappointment I felt. I would learn about some miracle remedy or modality with a mechanism of action that had helped many different children diagnosed with autism—but it wouldn't work for my Jack. This constant swinging back and forth between hope and disappointment wasn't just difficult. It was excruciating.

At times, it felt like torture.

The Possibilities of Autism

Unfortunately, *tortuous* could be a descriptor of our typical interactions with children with this condition. This was the case with a young boy from India named Tito. When he was five, he was brought to San Francisco to be evaluated by a panel of autism experts. He was placed in a room and given a straightforward assignment: he was to interpret a story that was read to him. He was asked by the man who was to read to him if he was ready to hear the story, and he acknowledged that he was. The man began reading.

When Tito was given a pencil and paper to complete his assignment, instead of writing about the story that was just read to him he wrote about other things entirely. He wrote about how beautiful the color green is and thoughts about sunshine on leaves.

When the evaluators saw what he wrote, they were confused. Why did he write what he did? Why didn't he listen to the passage? They became pretty frustrated when Tito was unable to comply with their requests.

Later, when Tito described the experience, he reported how his senses began to focus on the reader's voice more than his words. He saw the voice become long green- and yellow-colored strings. He said that the reader's voice formed threads like raw silk and then he watched those strings vibrate with different amplitudes as the reader varied his tones.

The experts thought he had failed to follow instructions. But he was fully engaged in this vibratory show of colors, strings, and threads. He hadn't interpreted the content of a story.

He had sensed beauty.

When he heard the speaker's voice, he was transported in his mind to a place where he could see the brilliant yellow light of the sun strike glistening green leaves and he became mesmerized by the wonder of it all.

It's a commonly held belief that a diagnosis of autism is a sentence of turmoil and despair for the child, the parent, and anyone else who cares about them. Some may look at children like Tito as the evaluators did, and think that they are incompetent because they are unable to pass the tests we set for them. With this perspective, we may even consider them mentally challenged and not teachable. I have written this book to suggest a different idea.

What the stories about Tito and Jack teach us is that a diagnosis of autism is not a life sentence of hopelessness, struggle, and despair. With a different mind-set about this admittedly complicated condition, we have the opportunity to learn about a whole new way to relate to the world. We have the chance to tap into a higher aspect of ourselves, to hear something as common as someone's voice reading a story and experience an exquisite beauty not typically discovered by most people. By knowing a child with autism, we have an opportunity to open ourselves up and reach for a life that far surpasses any previously held notions of what is possible. Such children open the door for us, should we choose to walk through it, to a life sentence not of turmoil and despair, but one of fulfillment and meaning. Through this diagnosis, we have the opportunity to live a life beyond what we ever imagined for ourselves and our child.

We have an opportunity to be awakened by autism and, in doing so, to help our children as well.

My son, who we were told might never reach out to us, is beginning to connect with us from a place deep inside himself. This is not because we have *trained* him to do so, but because he *wants* to. He truly desires the connection. And like Tito, I have seen him do remarkable things. He, like many other children with autism I have observed, has a brilliance about him that is typically assigned to the most enlightened, evolved individuals on the planet.

It is true that there is now an epidemic of autism populating our planet. I believe that our world has reached a critical threshold of toxicity, and the increasing number of diagnoses is the result. We can choose to see a strong message in this: a reflection of the amounts of stress, anxiety, and fear with which we have all been living. Something has got to give.

For many people, it feels natural to perceive a diagnosis of autism as a tragedy. But if we shift our beliefs about this condition and allow ourselves to see the brilliance in who our children are, then their health and well-being—as well as that of our families, and perhaps even our world—will improve beyond what we thought possible. The diagnosis can prove a powerful catalyst for this change.

Awakened by Autism has been written to help you see this possibility for yourself.

Getting the Most Out of This Book

Although I believe that this book can be helpful in expanding the understanding of anyone, *Awakened by Autism* offers much advice specifically directed toward the caretakers of children with autism. I have organized this book into two parts. Part I is about all the things that we can do to help a child achieve a balanced state of health. Though the underlying belief of this book is that these children are a source of brilliance, they do indeed have many obstacles to overcome in regard to their physical and mental well-being. I will take you through the process of understanding all of the pieces that might be out of balance in a child and how best to approach healing.

I believe that one of the tremendous gifts of our children is that they help us see a far greater beauty in the world around us; unfortunately, we may not necessarily be open to experiencing such things. So in the second part of this book, I address the opportunity that we have to align ourselves with our child's message and create a life of connection and meaning. I will take you through this process with the intention of helping you to expand your beliefs about what is possible for yourself as well as your child.

There is a better life to be had for our children diagnosed with autism, and there is a better way for us to live as well. We can do away with the fears and worries that accompany this diagnosis, and eliminate much of the unnecessary pain and suffering that we humans endure.

This is my hope—and why this book exists.

✦

Not long after the incident with the box of paint, Jack awoke at 5 A.M. and came into our bedroom to use our bathroom. He pretty much does this every morning. He sits in the bathroom where he has a few toys, usually some plastic cubes or pieces that he likes. He proceeds to drop them on the floor, over and over. He loves to listen to the sound of different shapes hitting the floor.

My poor husband, Pat, had been up working very late the night before, so this particular early morning was pretty hard for him. Jack was clanking away and squealing and squeaking, which he also likes to do. But at 5 A.M., it can be a bit much.

Pat jumped out of bed, went into the bathroom, and told Jack to stop.

"You're making too much noise, Jack," he grumbled. "Go back to bed."

And with that, Pat left and went downstairs to get what would be some much-needed coffee. I went into the bathroom to check on Jack.

I put my arm around him and asked if he was okay.

"Daddy's grumpy," he said.

"Yeah, he was up pretty late last night working," I told him. I felt so bad.

"Daddy's grumpy," Jack said again. "He's in pain. Want to give Daddy a kiss to make him feel better."

I sat back, stunned. It was one thing for Jack to want to kiss my face to make me better after a box of paint fell on me, but this was something else entirely. Most of us react when we're reprimanded. We get defensive. But not only had I never heard Jack articulate his understanding of another person's emotional state before; instead of getting defensive, he offered up a comforting response. He extrapolated the source of his father's anger and then overlooked it.

My ten-year-old boy with autism had just demonstrated to me what it meant to love.

Part One

INTERVENTION

Chapter One

THE PATH TOWARD BRILLIANCE

In the summer of 2004, we lived in the woods of Bridge-hampton, New York. At this time, my first son Jack was just six weeks old. One evening, my sister was visiting with her husband and son. At almost midnight, I slipped away to check on the baby. As a new mom, I didn't fully trust the baby monitor and needed the constant reassurance that he was still breathing. I went into the bathroom and flipped the light switch.

"AAAAAAAAAH!" I screamed.

My husband, Pat, as well as my sister suddenly arrived at the bedroom door.

"What is it?" Pat said. "It just sounded like you were attacked!"

"Bat," I whimpered, pointing to the rodent flying above our heads. Somehow it had found its way into the baby's room.

My husband managed to corner it and kill it, probably more from his own fear of the creature than any necessity to keep his family safe. He tossed it out into the woods and we had a good chuckle at all the drama we had found ourselves in at this late hour. We knew that the bat had been in our house for at least two nights, as my brother-in-law mentioned awakening the night before to a "big bird" flying around his room.

The next morning, I awoke with a nagging uncertainty. I had just finished my medical residency in emergency medicine the year before and I knew there were issues surrounding bat exposure and rabies. Namely, that rabies is 100 percent fatal, and bats' teeth are so small that a bite can be undetectable. However, further details were eluding me. I picked up the phone and called people from my training program to clarify, figuring that I would have to practice some sort of vaccination protocol. I was right; I was told I would have to vaccinate my infant son with a series of five rabies vaccines over the course of a month. So we embarked on that journey.

Jack was fine with the first three in the series. The fourth and fifth shots, however, caused seizure-like activity in him within 36 hours of each injection. At first, I did not make the connection between the vaccines and the seizures. But when it came time to administer his routine childhood vaccines, once again he had reactions 36 hours after the vaccination. Only this time, he continuously gasped and became rigid, flexing his knees to his chest and raising his arms straight up over his head while he slept. The pattern lasted the whole night.

We consulted with epilepsy specialists and determined it would be wise to delay any further vaccinations until after he was at least one year old. Before Jack had reached that age, I took him in for a well-baby visit. Of course, I relayed the advice of the specialists, and I was adamant about holding off on vaccines until a later date. I overheard the pediatrician say to his nurse that "the crazy mother thinks the vaccines caused a seizure in her son." I was livid, and switched pediatricians.

Jack continued to develop normally. When he was 17 months old, we took him for his first vaccine since the seizure episodes. I was apprehensive and uneasy about the visit, but I talked myself into the necessity of getting the diphtheria, tetanus, and pertussis vaccine (DTaP). I reasoned that, as a toddler, he might fall and cut himself frequently, and he should be protected against tetanus. The vaccine was only offered by combining the three together as a DTaP, so I chose this one to be the first.

At this age in Jack's life, he liked to talk. He had several words, some of which he repeated with tremendous enthusiasm because he loved our over-the-top excitement when he spoke. He regularly made eye contact with us, and aside from the rabies scare, he had passed all of his well-child visits without any problems. He was healthy, happy, and engaged.

Within a few days of the DTaP vaccine, my little boy disappeared. His face became sullen and gray. He had explosive diarrhea. He completely ignored us, like we did not exist. He began spending his entire day spinning the dog bowl or any other object he could spin. I lost my happy, healthy, engaged, and very much talking little boy to an expressionless child who withdrew into his own seemingly sad, uncomfortable world.

It would be another three months until I accepted that something was terribly wrong. I began the process of looking for answers, starting with a formal evaluation of Jack in our home with a county psychologist. I sat next to them on the floor as she spent several hours observing and evaluating him. At the end of this session, she handed me her report. On it was a rating scale for the continuum of symptoms relating to autism. On that scale, mild autism was rated around 20 and severe autism was around 40. I imagined that if anything, Jack might have mild autism—something that was entirely "fixable." I looked down at the paper.

She had rated him a *50.*

I cried every day for the next three weeks, all day and all night. I woke up sobbing in the middle of the night, overwhelmed that this nightmare was real and I could not escape it. But soon the futility of my despair gave way to a determination to find a way to help my boy. I made an appointment to see a pediatric developmental neurologist. Surely he would give me some answers and an action plan, right?

I felt optimistic when the day finally came for Jack's appointment. I had just finished reading my first book on autism recovery, which told the story of a mother who changed her son's diet and added some critical supplements. Fully armed with this information, we entered the pediatric neurologist's office.

"He is indeed severely autistic," the doctor said after observing him for a few minutes.

"I understand," I said. "What do you recommend we do?"

"There's not much you can do," he said.

I looked at him for a moment. *What?*

"Take him home and love him," he continued. "And someday, you should plan to institutionalize him, because there really is nothing that you can do. Of course, you can try applied behavior analysis, but the results are dismal at best."

"But what about diet?" I pleaded. "What about elimination diets and adding nutritional supplements?"

The doctor dismissed such methods, and reiterated that it would be best for us to prepare ourselves for the reality that he would never be able to care for himself or be educated in any meaningful way. I was devastated.

I took my son out of that room feeling completely defeated, but then something stirred in me as I left his office. I had this overwhelming feeling that this doctor was just plain wrong. I decided in that instant that I would search for the answers that this so-called expert had never bothered to investigate.

But what would I have to do to make this happen?

They Know Not What They Say

For many of us, finding out that our child is diagnosed with autism feels like a cancer diagnosis. We are completely yanked away from the life that was and suddenly given this new life instead. This new life might feel dark and hopeless and uncertain. I remember feeling like my life was over, that all the possibility for joy had disappeared. I was worried that my son's life was black and small and constricted. Like all that was possible for him was held inside a tiny, ugly little box.

I did not know much about autism when Jack was diagnosed. During medical school, my exposure to it was a five-minute video of a little boy rocking in a corner, isolated and withdrawn. We were told that if we saw one case of autism in our medical careers that would be a lot. So it makes sense that many physicians are limited in their knowledge about treatments.

My experience with the pediatric neurologist is an all too typical encounter. You may have been told something similar to what I was told, that autism is a lifelong condition with little hope for effective treatments. Perhaps you, like me, were given the recommendation to try applied behavior analysis (ABA); we dutifully put Jack in that therapy for years. This is often the only intervention recommended to parents, but the results can be equivocal and uninspiring.

You may have been told that children with autism get increasingly violent as they get older. You may have been told that some children need antipsychotic medication, or that they need to be institutionalized.

You have been given false information.

Some parents have shared with me how their pediatricians respond to the situation. "He is still your son," they are told. "You can still love him." They offer consolation rather than guidance, as if this somehow compensates for the meaningful treatment and direction they are never inclined to provide.

When I think about parents today receiving the same misdirection that I received in those first few weeks, I want to reach out to them through the cosmos with a big speaker and yell, "Do not listen to them! Do not listen to them! They know not what they say!!!"

I knew there had to be options so I began my search for answers. I went to autism conferences, met with autism experts, and I read anything I could that related to the issues surrounding autism. A couple of months after Jack's diagnosis, I took him to see a prominent autism physician, Dr. Sidney Baker. I was so impressed by this man's work that I then spent several years under his mentorship, learning all the details about the broken biochemistry of a diagnosed child as well as the treatment options available to repair these systems.

If there was a topic related to autism, I not only knew about it, I had probably met the practitioner or scientist who had developed the protocol. I became the walking encyclopedia of autism. Parents I met at workshops or conferences began to joke with me, attempting to come up with a therapy or topic that I hadn't tried.

I opened a private practice treating children with autism and sustained this practice for several years. I consulted with many different practitioners for my own son as well as for my patients. Through my work, I took note of how the patients responded to the efficacy of any given treatment plan. I saw transformation take place in my patients as well as my son, both in immediate response to some sort of action taken and through gradual improvements over time. And the more research I did, the more I became exposed to stories that the various modalities, therapies, and systems that were out there provided viable, sustainable change.

Through this immersion, I realized something incredibly important. An expert may have provided consolation to you in the form of a platitude like "He is still your son" or "You can still love him." You may have gotten the initial message, like I did, that everything in your child's world will only ever fit in a tiny, ugly little box. But in growing my understanding of the potential problems in the lives of children with autism, I'm here to tell you something different.

There is hope.

There is a path you can take to allow your child's brilliance to emerge.

One of the Most Complex Conditions on the Planet

There are many accounts of what is experienced by children with autism. One child perceived the patterns, colors, and minute details of the door, floor, windows, and curtains in the room in which he was situated. He received so much visual input that it became overpowering to the point that he could not initially recognize these structures for what they were. In other words, it took so much effort for the child to sift through all of the information he was receiving that he struggled to recognize that the door was just a door and that the window was just a window.

Some children are unable to recognize that their arms and legs are attached to their body. Others lose sight of where their limbs are in space. They describe the intense motion of the floor and the room, like they are swaying about at sea and unable to control the movement.

Children with autism tend to have a hypersensitive immune system, with clusters of symptoms manifesting as increased allergies, asthma, ear infections, and eczema. The immune system is tightly coupled to the digestive system, which is tightly coupled to the nervous system. The dysfunction of one system perpetuates dysfunction in another. Given this cascading effect, these children can be very uncomfortable in their own bodies. They develop digestive troubles, itchy skin, difficult breathing, and other manifestations of chronic illness. One teenage girl described her skin as feeling like there were thousands of fire ants crawling on her and biting her.

In 2007, a group of scientists set out to form a hypothesis surrounding the core pathology of an autistic brain. Through this study, they theorized that this pathology is hyperreactivity and hyperplasticity of local neuronal circuits. In other words, the neurons of the person with autism are processing information at highly excessive levels. This excessive processing may lead to hyperperception, hyperattention, and hypermemory, which they suggest may lie at the heart of most autistic symptoms. They labeled this alternative hypothesis the "intense world syndrome."

What is typically assumed about children with autism is that their disconnected, disengaged presence is the result of little functionality taking place in their brains. In the view of the intense world syndrome, however, the mechanism of dysfunction is one of *hyper*functionality. The authors of this study describe how the excessive amount of information these children take in becomes debilitating. Their hyperfunctionality may render the world painfully intense and even adversive, leading to social and environmental withdrawal. In order to cope, these children develop a small repertoire of behavioral routines that are obsessively repeated. When the children practice these routines, they're able to control the amount of input they receive. This is how they feel secure.

For many conditions and ailments, the recommended regimen is fairly straightforward and routine. Broken bones require certain protocols, as does the flu. But autism poses a unique medical challenge. The heightened neuronal function as well as the cascading dysfunction of the child's different physiological systems renders autism one of the most complicated disorders we have ever faced. The multifactorial causes of the child's discomfort and the innate complexity of each child's relationship to his own state of being not only make it a complicated problem to solve but a highly individualized undertaking as well.

There is a saying among some members of the medical community: "When you've seen one case of autism, you've seen one case." There are no two cases exactly alike. Yet if this is true, how are we supposed to respond?

There Is No Pill for Autism

As I've mentioned, I currently work as a medical doctor with a specialty in emergency medicine. When people come in to my hospital, having a stroke or heart attack, they need medication in order to live. They come in with their heads split open, needing stitches, or they have broken bones that need to be set. They suffer from overwhelming infections and metabolic crises requiring antibiotics and fluid resuscitation. They get shot and stabbed and need emergency surgery or other immediate, life-saving procedures. In this model, people come in broken and I can usually fix them.

Western doctors who are internists, pediatricians, or general practitioners are charged with the task of helping their patients to maintain wellness. However, their treatment methods emulate those of a doctor practicing emergency medicine. These doctors spend very little time with their patients and they are trained to intervene with a drug. Patients who have high blood pressure get a pill. Patients who have diabetes get a pill.

One could argue that doctors are now pushing lifestyle changes, like encouraging their patients to lose weight and eat better. And while this does happen to a certain degree, it goes against the grain of the Western model. Pharmaceutical companies drive medical research, which therefore means that the model supports the use of drugs. If an organization ran a study that proved eating more kale and taking calcium supplements lowers one's risk for osteoporosis, the pharmaceutical companies wouldn't be able to sell their product. The companies fund studies that prove that their drug will lower blood pressure. The Western medical model so often supports business over wellness, which is the antithesis of why I began practicing medicine in the first place.

In hindsight, I chose emergency medicine as my specialty because it allows me to practice Western medicine while remaining aligned with my values. I find it acceptable to prescribe pharmaceuticals in response to strokes and metabolic crises because emergencies require this type of intervention. Of course, everyone must choose for themselves whether the cost-benefit ratio of pharmaceuticals is acceptable in their own case.

Though most doctors support this model, it's not really their fault that the infrastructure of Western medicine is driven by business as much as it is. Health insurance companies dictate medical coverage, and the enormity and power of pharmaceutical companies drive treatment options. Doctors are part of a system that is set up to work exactly as it does and they're provided with very little incentive to work outside of this process.

It will therefore be not at all surprising that doctors look at the symptoms of autism exactly like they look at any other disease or disorder. If a child with autism has attention problems, he might be prescribed Ritalin or Adderall. If a child has anxiety or appears depressed, he might be prescribed an antidepressant like Paxil or Prozac. I was blown away recently when a colleague asked me if I knew the dose of the antidepressant Zoloft for a seven-year-old. A study was conducted in 2007 that revealed a patient who had taken sertraline (the generic term for Zoloft) had suicidal thoughts. Do we really want to give this type of drug to a seven-year-old?

One patient who I treated in the emergency room was extremely fearful and paranoid. He was having a psychotic break and hearing voices. When it was time for me to perform a physical exam, he wasn't even able to sit still. I prescribed Risperdal, an antipsychotic medication, to calm him down and sedate him enough so he was no longer a danger to himself. I was then able to examine him and get him admitted to the hospital.

The problem is, doctors prescribe Risperdal to children with autism as well.

Once again, this is understandable, as risperidone (Risperdal) and aripripazole (Abilify) are the only two FDA-approved drugs for treating autism. But children with autism aren't psychotic. And just because prescribing drugs is a function of our medical infrastructure, does that mean that it's the correct approach?

When we prescribe antipsychotic drugs for autism, it often means that we are focusing on treating the symptoms alone. Yet when we do this, we miss the opportunity for wellness. If your roof has a leak and it rains, your bedroom gets wet. If you place a bucket under the hole, your bedroom will remain dry temporarily. You are essentially treating the symptom, which is a wet bedroom. But if you look for the cause, which is a hole in the roof, you can repair the roof and remain symptom-free. Which method would be the most effective? The one in which you have to keep replacing buckets, risk mold buildup around the hole, and generally keep managing the problem? Or the one in which the problem is resolved permanently?

It is for this reason that treating autism with drugs is not effective. Furthermore, the one main behavior therapy that is funded by school districts and the government is ABA, and this also takes a symptoms-elimination approach. If a child with autism is stimming (self-stimulating) in a way that is not socially accepted, such as flapping his hands or rocking repetitively, an ABA practitioner might seek to eliminate this behavior without understanding the cause. This leads to a lost opportunity for wellness, and damage might be done to the relationship between the child and his parents as well as other caretakers.

Autism presents in each child differently. And because of this, we are presented with a unique and complicated problem for healing not only the physical symptoms but also for addressing the emotional and spiritual needs of the child. But if the scope of Western medicine's symptom-based approach lacks the tools we need, what is the alternative?

Treating Every Child as an Individual

As I've mentioned, I began a private practice treating children with autism in 2008. I was mentored by Dr. Sidney Baker, the grandfather of the alternative biomedical movement for autism, and after that I saw many children.

Some months after starting the practice, I found myself feeling extremely fatigued to the point that I thought I had cancer. But soon enough, I learned that I wasn't dying of cancer—I was pregnant again. This was a surprise because after my second child Sam was born in 2005, when I was in my early 40s, I thought having another baby at this age was too big a risk and I'd had my tubes tied! When we discovered our good fortune, we moved forward with total joy. In April of 2009, my youngest son, Ben—our miracle baby—was born.

I continued to run my private practice with my third baby and I also continued to work one shift per week in the emergency room. After attempting to juggle all of these responsibilities for a while, I decided to close the practice and focus more on my family. I worked out a plan with each patient's family and referred each child to a practitioner who I thought could continue our work.

Two children from my practice, Peter and Maria, stand out to me the most. Peter was four years old when I first met him. He spoke only in single words, no sentences. He showed no interest in people and he spent most of his days in his own world perseverating on trucks and lining them up. He went to a special school at the time because his parents were told that early intervention was the key to progress. Maria was five years old when I met her and she was a little whirlwind. She never sat still and I remember her bouncing around the office, walking on her tippy toes and flapping her hands. She had no interest in her siblings or her parents, and she was perfectly content to be by herself all day long. She also went to a special school for children with autism.

Recently, Peter's mother reached out to me via e-mail and had this to say:

> Peter has been recovered from autism for a little over four years, and it's amazing how time flies. He continues to thrive and loves school. He is actually an amazing artist and loves to write and illustrate short stories and has

best friends. The only "autism" remnant that remains is minimal stimming, which at this point makes Peter who he is: a unique boy.

I also ran into Maria's mother at the grocery store about a year ago. She came up to me with such exuberance that I got a little nervous. "Oh, Dr. Libutti, do you remember me?" she said. "I am Maria's mother and we used to see you. I just want to thank you. Maria goes to school now, and she is so smart and has lots of friends. I just want to thank you so much for helping us!"

In both cases, these children are now nearly free of many of the most severe symptoms and negative behaviors associated with autism. They have meaningful relationships that they played an active role in cultivating. What was done to get these results? What got these children to emerge so brilliantly from their original diagnoses?

When I worked with him, Peter had been improving nicely with dietary changes and specific supplements that supported his special physiological needs. When I closed my practice, I referred him to a practitioner who specialized in homotoxicology. Maria suffered from extreme allergic reactions to certain substances, so I referred her to a physician in Long Island who specializes in autism with a background in allergies and immunology.

These were two children who both suffered from having broken physiology, and they both had problems with their immune, digestive, and nervous systems, but they were entirely different in the way these problems manifested.

Having attended dozens of autism conferences and met a majority of the autism experts, I have witnessed the promotion of specific modalities, each one promising to be *the* "silver bullet" that will cure autism. While numbers of children have improved greatly with each of these specific modalities, I have learned that the best approach is something different.

Peter and Maria didn't improve because of a cure-all, silver-bullet-like remedy. They did so because their parents implemented a regimen specific to their particular needs.

If a child is participating in a seemingly odd behavior, like hand flapping, toe walking, or lining up toys, there is nothing inherently wrong with the child. He is merely behaving in a way that enables him to make sense of his world and take care of himself. He may be experiencing an extreme sensitivity to visual stimuli, and the hand flapping soothes the discomfort. I know of one boy who described the feeling of unfiltered light penetrating like sharp, hot needles to his eyes, but when he flapped his fingers and hands in front of his face he filtered the light and soothed the pain. Not only is there nothing wrong with these behaviors, but the specific nature of these behaviors demonstrates the specific nature of these children's discomfort as well.

If the Western approach of responding to autism is like sticking a bucket under a leak in the roof, then fixing the roof itself equates to addressing the child's needs as an individual. Rather than simply administering pills, we determine the underlying cause of the child's symptoms and uncomfortable behaviors. Peter and Maria made wondrous strides because we treated the whole child. We addressed the needs of not just these children's bodies but their minds and spirits as well.

The Western medical approach to illness and disease is notorious for focusing on curbing the symptoms. But by understanding the whole child, we can create an intervention plan that supports and heals holistically.

When we take a holistic approach and consider mind, body, and spirit, we allow the child's own innate ability to heal to take over. However, this is almost never cut-and-dried. Autism requires a comprehensive approach that often includes a variety of different modalities, and redirection of the treatment plan is common.

How do we implement such a multifaceted approach? My mentor, Dr. Baker, used to tell parents who were overly interested in running laboratory tests that the best test was the "thumbs" test. That meant doing a treatment trial and letting the child give us an answer. If the child made substantial progress, we gave "two thumbs up." If not, we gave "two thumbs down." It has repeatedly demonstrated itself as an effective way to approach a complicated situation. It was what I did to determine that Peter needed to undergo homotoxicology as well as timeline sequential therapy. It was how we determined that Maria should see the physician who specializes in allergies and immunology.

Children with autism are like an enigma. When we approach their lifestyle methodically and with love, acceptance, and wonder, we can help them return to their natural state of well-being. We are all born with unique gifts to share with the world, but children with autism need a radically different approach to enable their brilliance to emerge. I remember Peter and Maria's parents to be extremely optimistic and accepting of their children. This is a crucial point to be made in regard to the outcome they experienced. The healing process encompasses not just the physical but the emotional and spiritual aspects of the child and his environment.

We will explore these various components throughout this book. I will walk you through a process to help you create a lifestyle and environment that supports your children so they can begin to feel more comfortable in their bodies and more trusting of their environment. If we accept and embrace them exactly where they are and seek to understand their world, we will inspire them to venture out of their own world and join us in ours.

The first few months after his slip into autism, Jack was especially sick. He had no interest in his family. He just wanted to spin the dog's water bowl. The pictures we have of Jack on his second birthday show a completely disinterested little boy who was oblivious to the party, the cake, and the presents. He never smiled and he completely stopped talking.

His progress in that first year was slow moving. I recorded every little improvement or regression. I would write things like "Jack seemed more connected today" or "Jack was stimming like crazy, totally disconnected and lost." I would report on the state of his bowel movements, always searching for improvement and relief from the chronic, relentless diarrhea that plagued him. I searched for any sign that he might one day speak again. Very little happened, but despite a lack of such indicators, we continued to try new diets, supplements, and other modalities that seemed like they might be of help.

One day, about ten months after Jack's diagnosis, we were about to have dinner. I had been preparing food in the kitchen, and Jack was in the family room where I could see him spinning his toys. In those days, I was always trying to promote Jack's speech, so I went over to him, picked up a blue ball, and asked him what color it was.

Jack didn't look up at me. He was seemingly oblivious to my question, and even to the fact that I was in the room with him at all. I put the ball down and started walking back to the kitchen.

"Blue."

I looked up. Jack had identified the object as blue and said the word. After, he went right back to spinning his toy. But when I realized what had happened—that Jack had said his very first word since his decline one year prior—I enjoyed my happiest moment since his diagnosis. Perhaps it really was possible that Jack could improve.

Now, I had hope.

🧩 🧩 🧩

Chapter Two

THE UNIQUE PHYSIOLOGY OF AUTISM

"There is a reason why children with autism struggle as they do."

I looked up at the presenter, alongside all of the other members of the audience. Would this reason she spoke of coincide with all the research I had been doing myself?

"And that reason," she continued, "is cerebral hypoperfusion."

At this time, it had been a year and a half since Jack's initial diagnosis. Meanwhile, I had immersed myself in learning about every kind of biomedical modality that I could find in the hopes that one of them would be the key to his condition. In these early days, I was very focused on finding a "cure" for Jack. This included reading all sorts of books, watching DVDs, and attending conferences. I learned about the nature of inflammation in the child's brain, how the child's immune system could be greatly compromised, and other maladies. And, I had also learned about cerebral hypoperfusion, which was a medical term for decreased blood flow to the brain.

I was now at a conference that featured a lecture on hyperbaric oxygen therapy (HBOT), which was the act of entering a pressurized chamber and breathing in oxygen. As the presenter spoke, all of these light bulbs were going off in my brain about the significance of decreased blood flow to the brains of children with autism.

The presenters talked about studies that confirmed this diminished blood flow in the brains of these children and how this impairment seriously affected their ability to speak and focus their attention. They went on about the promise of HBOT, which very simply increased blood flow to the brain and reversed this problem.

I was hooked. I made a beeline to the HBOT booth after the lecture and took a test drive. It was pretty far out. I crawled into the top of this long tube and they zipped the chamber shut. I felt like an astronaut entering a simulator. After I was hooked up to an oxygen concentrator, I laid back and enjoyed the hum. It was cool. But, more significantly, I believed in the science behind it.

When I got out, I was so elated I couldn't wait to tell my husband and my friend Susan—I called them both immediately. Susan was at home and liked to hear about interesting therapies as soon as I discovered them. She was the mother of an autistic child, like me, and she listened with enthusiasm as I spewed out the details so fast I probably scared her. We were going to do this and I felt sure it could be the solution I was looking for.

I made arrangements to rent a chamber as soon as I got home, and so did Susan. When it arrived I set it up and had it running that night. It looked like a tubular tent with a metal frame and heavy blue fabric, with a large zipper running the length of the chamber. I set up a little cozy play area for Jack with a pillow, blankets, and books. We had to go in twice a day for 90 minutes each, so we needed to be comfortable and have stuff to do.

It took two people to get this thing going. I would crawl in with Jack after turning on the oxygen concentrator and Pat would zip us in. I could sit up without difficulty so it became a fun little ritual. In the morning we climbed in with books and games and in the evening we went in after dinner and bath time so Jack could fall asleep in there. Pat would unzip us quietly, I would lift my sleeping boy up to him, and he would carry Jack to bed.

These sessions were called "dives." The protocol was to conduct dives twice a day for 45 days; then we would take 30 days off. After about a month, some really beautiful things happened. I fondly remember hanging out with Jack in the den as we sat on the sofa. While before these dives he generally seemed disengaged and unfocused, after we began the protocol he began looking at me and smiling. He seemed so cheery and far more connected than he ever had before.

I took tons of pictures of him that month. Usually, he would look through the camera, as if it were just another one of the many objects that surrounded him at that moment in time. But after we began HBOT, he actually looked at the camera itself. He was happy.

I was convinced there was something to this therapy, so I took out a loan and bought a chamber. It cost $20,000, but I didn't care—I had to have one.

During the recommended 30-day break between therapies, Jack turned four. We moved into a new home, set up the hyperbaric chamber, and chose a school district that would provide the support he needed in the classroom. However, in the process of the move, Jack somehow slipped back into his old ways. He stopped smiling as much, and his connection to us faded. I wondered if he shut down in response to the stress of moving.

Our first dive in the new house felt good because it enabled us to be proactive again, but the atmosphere during this round of therapy felt somehow muted. I wondered why Jack did not maintain lasting benefit. How could he do so beautifully, lose his gains, and then not recover them? Was there some unknown cascade of molecular physiology that prevented him from holding the benefit? But whatever the reason was for this regression, there was one thing of which I was definitely sure.

Hyperbaric oxygen therapy was not the solution I had hoped it would be.

The Problem with Silver Bullets

When I bought the HBOT chamber, I was very invested in the belief that there was a cure for my son. I was learning everything I could about the physiological dysfunction inherent to children with autism, and I was certain I could figure it out. Something was broken—surely I could find a way to correct it, right?

The chamber is only one example of the many things I did in my determination to "fix" my son; it was definitely the most costly. Not only did I invest money, I also invested a great deal of energy and hope. I bought into the idea that this modality was "the one." And, like so many other modalities that I made such a big investment in, it didn't wind up being the silver bullet that I thought it would be. The real downside to all of these supposed cures was the heavy disappointment, over and over, when the results did not pan out. HBOT was especially hard because I did see amazing results early on; however, they faded and did not readily return.

This story is a perfect example of how my mind-set operated back then. After all, I was trained in a United States medical school. My training required us to study distinct subjects, including neurology, immunology, endocrinology, and every other organ system—and each of these subjects was examined in a separate course. There was never a convergence of systems into the whole human being that we are. When we graduate from medical school, we choose a specialty and the model perpetuates itself.

Because of this divergent approach to the human body, we are continually exposed to the silver-bullet mind-set for practicing medicine. Going to see a general practitioner when something is wrong will likely get us sent on to see a specialist. If we have high blood pressure, we see a cardiologist. If we have diabetes, we see an endocrinologist. If we have chronic headaches, we see a neurologist, and so on. And what most likely happens when we see the specialist? We get put on a medication to control the specific symptoms they specialize in that are making us uncomfortable. This might include administering a quick-fix type of solution, like if a patient complains of back pain and their doctor prescribes painkillers and muscle relaxants. But it can also include administering a more permanent solution, as might be the case with a patient taking blood pressure medication for a lengthy period of time. The problem with this approach is that this never gets to the cause of our symptoms and a person might end up on drug after drug—often with serious side effects.

We have all been exposed to drug company television commercials where the benefits of a drug are touted in the first 15 seconds and then the last 45 seconds are spent warning about the possible side effects. Taking a drug to ameliorate one symptom but having side effects like nausea, dizziness, blood clots, or headaches is not the path to wellness that we need. I am frequently dumbfounded in the emergency room when I see someone who takes 20 or 30 different medications in one day. The more we consider the Western view of the body as a series of separate, distinct systems, the more we miss huge opportunities for healing.

So it is no surprise that medical professionals have a limited perspective from which to approach autism. Unfortunately, mainstream medicine views autism as a psychiatric illness. It is classified in the *Diagnostic and Statistical Manual of Mental Disorders* (DSM-5), which is the reference manual mental-health physicians use to diagnose mental disorders in the United States. So it follows that the only two FDA-approved drugs for autism are both antipsychotic drugs.

However, my silver-bullet mentality also arose from my exposure to many professionals promoting their therapy as *the* therapy. I got wrapped up in the HBOT rush because I believed that autism could be cured with one modality—if only I could figure out *which* one. But the physiology of a child with autism is affected in so many ways by so many things. It's not just a simple condition in need of a certain drug or procedure; it's a total biochemical train wreck. It's not a fill-in-the-blank exercise; it's a complicated puzzle.

Within the Western medical community, there are indeed a number of medical practitioners who are focused on a specific area of expertise regarding the treatment of autism. They are typically focused on one aspect of the body because they have had success with some children in their practice using a particular therapy. For example, some practitioners are focused on the immune system, while others help the child with detoxification. While this approach is not ideal, I am grateful that these practitioners exist because they at least provide solutions to aspects of the autism puzzle.

These biomedical practitioners provide a starting place for interested parties to further their knowledge. It is from them that I have learned so many of the details of all that goes into addressing autism as a condition. But because of the biochemical train wreck of autism, I have learned something else as well.

I've learned that looking for the silver bullet is futile.

Why the Biochemical Train Wreck?

We bring our typical children to the doctor for one of two reasons. The first reason is that our child is sick with some sort of ailment, whether it's minor symptoms like a cold, a rash, or vomiting, or any one of the typical childhood illnesses like the flu or impetigo. We expect to get a prescription for an antibiotic or reassurance that the illness will run its course and our child will be fine. The other reason, at least during the first two years of life, is a routine checkup, like a well-baby visit. Our child is measured, weighed, and looked at, and at times given vaccinations.

When we bring our child with autism to the doctor, there is very little difference in this routine, with the exception of a discussion about behavior problems or any "autistic-like" anxiety, aggression, or hyperactivity. In cases of behavior issues that are seen as out of control, the doctor may prescribe an antipsychotic, or perhaps antianxiety or antidepressant medication. The doctor may even refer the child to a psychiatrist.

The process for treating ailments in the body is identical to the way adults are managed in this medical model. We see a specialist to manage the system that is acting up and we are treated for an isolated organ system. Similarly, if the child with autism has severe gastrointestinal issues like chronic diarrhea or constipation, the doctor will refer the child to a gastroenterologist. If the child shows signs of allergies or asthma, the doctor will refer the child to an allergist or pulmonologist. It is likely that once the specialist sees the child, some medication will be prescribed to reduce the symptoms. But what is rarely taken into consideration with adults or children in this model is the fact that the body's systems are exquisitely intertwined. What affects one affects another.

To understand the body and its interconnectedness, we have to consider the carefully orchestrated dance between the digestive system, immune system, nervous system, and detoxification system. These are the big players in autism that deserve special attention. However, we cannot ignore that the rest of the body's systems all play a role in the return to balance as well.

We can consider the digestive system as the major headquarters for the immune and nervous systems. Within the gastrointestinal (GI) tract, there are a variety of beneficial bacteria, specialized immune cells, and a complex network of neurological and hormonal components. The GI tract is home to 70 percent of the body's immune system and it contains the body's largest concentration of mood-altering neurotransmitters like serotonin.

There is substantial biochemical signaling that takes place between the GI tract and the nervous system. Much of this process is facilitated by intestinal bacteria, called microbiota, which have been shown to play an important role in healthy brain function. The significance of this concentration of signaling, referred to as the gut-brain axis, is substantiated by an abundance of research currently being pursued in the autism medical community.

Often, a specific system of the body will be thrown off balance in response to certain conditions. When this happens, it can trigger a domino effect that then affects many of the other systems. This forms the basis of the biochemical train wreck, and is exactly what happens in a child with autism. The nervous system might be damaged by an infection or toxin, or the immune system can become impaired by some insult. It's difficult to say for sure where the cascade begins. But regardless of its origin, the effect is a vicious cycle that is perpetuated until some intervention can slow it down and allow the body to return to balance.

We know that children with autism typically suffer from neuroinflammation, which is a process that is caused by a dysfunctional immune response and affects brain function. We see a higher proportion of seizures in children with autism. We see sensory imbalances like hypersensitivity to sound, touch, and all the other senses. We see vestibular dysfunction, which controls coordination and balance and is linked to neuroinflammation in the cerebellum. And the developmental delays in children with autism, including speech, language, and social impairment, can all be traced to abnormal brain physiology.

The immune system also plays a role in the allergic symptoms that often plague children with autism. There are higher incidences of asthma, food and airborne allergies, skin rashes like eczema, chronic ear infections, and even autoimmune responses to brain proteins.

The digestive system, hosting much of the immune system, is also clearly affected and often damaged in children with autism. The microvilli of the gut mucosa are damaged and blunted, causing large proteins to cross into the bloodstream. This in turn puts the immune system on overdrive. So the child has an ongoing, self-perpetuating cycle of poor absorption of needed nutrients while unwanted proteins pass into the blood and cause continued stress on the immune system. These systems are so tightly coupled that we cannot address one without addressing the other.

When we understand that there are many points of entry of dysfunction—that there are so many different ways that a child can have his own unique biochemical train wreck—we can see why no two children with autism can be treated exactly the same. This is the reason there is no one-size-fits-all approach and why we cannot treat the child through an "isolated systems" perspective.

We need to consider a different approach instead.

The Importance of Cause and Effect

During my private practice, I saw one little boy with very little language. He was barely able to put two words together to form simple sentences, and usually just refrained from speaking at all. I prescribed him a supplement called methyl B_{12}, which was administered through injections. Methylation is a key biochemical process that is essential for proper function of almost all of our body's systems. Research has found a positive correlation between the impairment of methylation and inflammation of the brain, so administering methyl B_{12} activates a biochemical pathway that ultimately gives more fuel to the brain's matter. Many children with autism suffer from inflammation, and some of them do show improvements using these injections—like gaining a few new words here and there. But this particular boy? After receiving the injections, he began speaking whole sentences.

I saw a different young boy who had been suffering from chronic diarrhea with a bloated belly and severe sleep problems. He looked malnourished despite the bloated belly, and he failed to gain weight. His arms and legs were thin, and he slowly fell off the pediatric growth chart (the tool pediatricians use to plot the height and weight of children). We put him on a diet called the specific carbohydrate diet (SCD). It eliminates not just gluten and casein but all grains and complex carbohydrates. After being on this diet for one year, the boy slept through the night and gained five pounds. But even more encouraging (though sleeping through the night is enough for most parents), he began to progress in school. He wrote legibly for the first time and he was more focused and able to learn.

Although both children likely shared certain derangements in their immune system, nervous system, digestive system, and detoxification system, their specific biochemical makeup was as different as their fingerprints. Methylation is almost certainly impaired in many children with autism, but it may not be the main thing that derails your child as it did for the child in my first example. Eliminating foods that promote inflammation was what helped the second boy's inflamed lining of the gut mucosa begin to heal.

Why did the two boys improve so dramatically from two completely different modalities? The answer is simple: the interventions administered for any given child should be formulated based on their individual needs.

Many people who have had success with a particular modality might declare that it is the ideal solution for every other child as well. They honestly believe they have the silver bullet to "cure" all kids with autism. But as the stories of these two boys show us, each child has specific problems with his own individual physiology that needs a specific type of intervention. As such, each child needs to have his own individual plan.

We don't just treat individual symptoms. We treat the whole child.

Essentially, treating the whole child consists of regarding his unique physiology as its own story that needs to be considered as a stand-alone narrative. As we explored in the previous section, one child's original imbalance might be very different from another child's, and we need to look at the various clues that particular child's body leaves us to determine what must be done in response.

While doing this can seem overwhelming and quite complicated, it is definitely possible. A typical person who desires to become healthier and fitter might try out different diets, supplements, and even exercise regimens to help him optimize his health in a way that suits his lifestyle, body type, and personality. Some things work really well for him, while others—not so much. But this process also forms the basis of how to develop a plan of intervention for a child with autism. This is a process we more commonly refer to as "trial and error."

Finding Physical Balance Through Experimentation

During my own process of trial and error, I remember trying to get B vitamins into Jack early on. Vitamin B_6 used to be very popular because it appeared to be extremely beneficial for children with autism and the science to support this was very strong. I tried many different forms of B_6 but Jack was just not able to tolerate it.

Jack and I went to Seattle, where we saw a very popular holistic doctor who had been working with children with autism. He told us that Jack was particularly deficient in vitamin B_6, and Jack received an oral dose of liquid B_6 just before we headed to the airport to fly home. Within about two hours of the B_6 dose, I watched my boy become what I can only describe as psychotic.

He tensed his entire body, his heart raced, his pupils dilated, and he had this wild look in his eyes. He also clenched his teeth and ground them with such intensity I thought they would break. I was really scared. I brought him into the tiny airplane bathroom and I just held him and cried. I tried to comfort him and soothe him, through my tears, and eventually I brought him back to our seat. The B_6 wore off later that day and I was not able to give him B vitamins until several years later.

Each child's biochemistry is so unique that even within a category of supplements, like B vitamins, the outcome can be wildly different from one child to the next. Some children might thrive in response to the supplement that doctor administered, while others could have the opposite reaction like Jack did.

The complicated nature of autism and the individuality of each child drives the trial-and-error process that is required when formulating a plan for healing. And though the process may be customized to any given child, its main goals are fairly consistent: to heal the digestive system, balance the immune system, and reduce brain inflammation. We also want to pay special attention to the child's impaired detoxification system.

Given all of this, my goal here is not to offer a one-size-fits-all plan but rather to guide you through a protocol that involves your own experimentation. This approach is necessitated by the requirements of educating a large group with diverse physiology. While Jack has a unique makeup of biochemical imbalances, what worked for him may or may not work for others. I have seen this to be true with all of the children I treated in my private practice. Many parents ask about lab testing, hoping there are special tests that will give them hard-and-fast answers. Unfortunately, there are few tests that can effectively guide decisions about therapy.

This means that the best starting place is unique to each child. I was trained with a physician who always liked to approach a child with a best guess about where to start, based on the child's history and a physical exam. Parents are the child's best resource because they are most aware of the most pressing issues. In my private practice, I always wanted to know what the most challenging issue was so we could address this first. There are a number of possibilities.

A child might have chronic, watery diarrhea and fail to gain weight. If this is the most troubling issue to the parent, it is a good indicator that the digestive system is an ideal starting place. Experimenting with a gluten-free and casein-free (GF/CF) diet or an even more restrictive diet like the Specific Carbohydrate Diet seems reasonable. I would advise the parents to be supervigilant with the diet for a short period of time, maybe three to four weeks. This is usually enough time to see a response, if there is going to be one. The next decision is made after this trial period.

Another child might suffer from severe allergies, have bad eczema, have dark circles under the eyes, or suffer from a chronically runny nose. For this child, we might begin with immune strengthening supplements in addition to eliminating allergens from the diet (using an allergy elimination diet to uncover hidden allergies). I would also recommend eliminating any obvious allergy triggers around the house and perhaps recommend using a HEPA air filter in the bedroom.

Another child might be completely off balance, with frequent falls. I remember a child who fell so much as a toddler that we had to put a helmet on him to protect his brain from trauma. While all children require a comprehensive approach, this child's neuro-inflammation was the priority so we began with strong antioxidants and some alternative modalities as well. I find that children with strong indicators of excessive neuroinflammation, like a child with frequent seizures or the clumsy toddler mentioned above, will benefit early on from specifically seeking greater balance in the brain.

A child who is showing excessive sensory integration problems would benefit from a different starting point. If the parents cannot take the child out in public because sound is so overwhelming, then this becomes the most important first step. There are sensory environments that can calm hyperactive sensory systems. But it is also likely that some trial and error with diet and supplements would be initiated early on.

If a parent reports that their child never gets sick and has never had a fever, then I become concerned about the inability of the immune system to mount a response. The child may not have had colds, flus, or fevers, but perhaps he is severely delayed in speech. He may have sallow, gray skin and look sickly. These children are often severely immune compromised and they may benefit from a rigorous detoxification protocol that involves special emphasis on cleaning out heavy metals or other toxins that are stuck in their body. Again, this may be a great place to start, with other interventions added as we gain traction on moving some of the toxins out of their system.

There are many diets that can address specific issues. Besides GF/CF, SCD, and allergy elimination diets, there are diets that reduce salicylate and phenolic compounds (e.g., the Feingold diet) that are troublesome in some children.

The list of supplements is enormous and can be very overwhelming. However, we always have a place to start and we move forward systematically as based on the child's response. Like a tailored diet, adding supplements will be individualized but most children with autism will benefit from some starter supplements.

I have found methyl B_{12} injections to be very useful in severely speech-delayed children. I have also found different forms of omega fatty acids to be powerful, like Speak by NourishLife, a real game changer for Jack as he continued to develop his language. I also recommend using phosphatidylcholine (PC), a phospholipid and vital component of the cell membrane. Patricia Kane, Ph.D., has a protocol that is worth looking into; her PC products, made by BodyBio, are the best in their class. I love using wholefood supplements like chlorella because they are easily assimilated and packed with nutrients. I also recommend a good probiotic in most children (like Theralac by Master Supplements), a multimineral (like BrainChild Nutritionals), a multivitamin if tolerated, and, for some children, digestive enzymes (like those by the brand Enzymedica). You can see the Resources section at the back of this book for some of my suggestions.

I would even recommend exploring hyperbaric oxygen therapy in some cases. There are HBOT clinics springing up all over the country for this purpose, and there is very little downside to doing a trial. Jack's initial gains may have abated, but the upside for some children can be substantial.

The parents should always provide their input, as they often have gut feelings about certain modalities or may be drawn to a particular therapy. I always listen to a parent's intuition.

There are so many promising interventions when we look at the child's body from a biomedical standpoint. There are always clues as to which approach to begin with, but the ongoing process is usually trial and error. Finding physical balance within the biological framework of a child with autism is one of the most complex medical processes in existence. But great strides can be made with persistent effort and guidance from a qualified practitioner. Jack may not have responded well to that B_6 supplement, but through trial and error we eventually determined which supplements were ideal for his particular physiology.

When I came to the conclusion that HBOT would not be the silver bullet I had hoped for, I found the next hot intervention—chelation administered by IV. Chelation is a process of introducing a chelating agent (like edetic acid, EDTA) into the bloodstream so that it can grab heavy metals like mercury, lead, and aluminum.

Knowing what I know now, I would not recommend IV chelation for any child. I believe that it is too hard on the body and there are more gentle approaches to assist the body in eliminating heavy metals and other toxins. I find that it is ideal to avoid any modalities that are invasive in general.

When I first began chelation with Jack, I thought we made some nice progress. He was more connected and his language improved. After about four months, though, he began to regress. He developed diarrhea and dark circles under his eyes, and his general appearance was dull. His language faded to some degree and he became disconnected again.

One day, I noticed that the collar of one of his shirts was all chewed up. On another day, it was the ends of his sleeves. Then, the bottom of the shirt. Eventually, he destroyed his shirt by the end of each day.

Obviously, this was a red flag.

I knew that *pica,* a term that describes eating inedible items, was prevalent among children in underprivileged countries due to their suffering from malnutrition. The child intuitively searches for a much-needed nutrient. It was obvious in Jack's case that, through the chelation, I had depleted valuable nutrients like calcium and magnesium. It took about a month to replenish these minerals with a high daily dose of a multimineral.

This incident brought home for me the realization that my silver-bullet approach was not working. I would have to move forward in a different way.

Chapter Three

OVERCOMING TOXICITY

In March 2007, we were still living in our house in Bridge-hampton, NY—the same house that had the bat in it almost three years earlier. We were one year into Jack's diagnosis and were concerned about his health. He had recurrent infections and severe asthma attacks on a very frequent basis.

I had to repeatedly take Jack to a walk-in clinic for nasal cultures. His sinus-related symptoms were constant and he always cultured positive for some nasty infections. We hated to put him on antibiotics, but the severity of the infections and the invasive nature of the bacteria that grew out motivated me to keep medicating him.

He also suffered from very frequent, severe asthma attacks. I had asthma when I was a child, but never to the degree that Jack was experiencing symptoms. As a trained emergency physician, I could treat severe asthma attacks with my eyes closed. But when Jack had an attack, I freaked out. They were that scary.

This was during the time in which I worked as an apprentice to Sid Baker to develop my expertise as an autism-centric physician. But Sid was also Jack's doctor. One day, I was discussing the ongoing infections and asthma with Sid on the phone.

"Andie," he said, "I'm coming over. I'll be right there."

Sid lived only about ten minutes away, and I was thrilled that he wanted to help me.

"Great," I said. "See you in a few minutes."

When Sid arrived, he walked through the front door and said hello. Then he took a big, long sniff.

"You've got a really bad mold problem," he said.

"I do?"

"Yes, really bad. Show me where Jack sleeps," he added.

I took him to the back bedroom where Jack slept. The house was built on a sloping grade, and the slope of a big hill ran downstream directly into the house at his bedroom. While we did not have any leaks, the poor design of this structure invariably led to a moisture problem.

As we looked around, I realized that some of the shoes in the closet had a fine, fuzzy dusting of mold. And this was an active, used closet, not a storage closet. It was really bad.

Sid and I just looked at each other in disbelief. He then went on to describe possibilities to remedy the problem, like an elaborate ventilation system in the crawl space and other options. But none of these solutions seemed financially feasible to us.

"Look," he said, "call a mold remediator and get them out here to test the place and then figure out your options. If you can't resolve the issue, come live in our cottage; it's empty until the summer. You can't keep Jack in this house the way it is now. He'll never get better."

And with that, he left.

I had a mold tester out the next day. He took out his collecting tools and took samples from the air. He rubbed swabs on the fuzzy shoes and took swabs of areas of the house that were likeliest to pose a problem. When he left, he told me he'd be in touch in a few days.

I got the call within 48 hours.

"You have *Stachybotrys chartarum*," he said. "That's the worst toxic black mold you can have. You have other bad molds growing, but this one is really bad."

Crap. Now what was I going to do? I got online and looked at all the possible effects of Stachybotrys: respiratory problems, skin inflammation, mental fog, immune-system suppression, and many more. Jack had exhibited many of these symptoms. "That's it," I said to Pat. "We are moving out." And we did. We moved into Sid's cottage that night. Me, Pat, Jack, Sam, and our golden retriever, Jake. I was overwhelmed and sick to my stomach, but also relieved. Jack's chronic infections and asthma seemed very likely to be connected to the mold. Now we could move forward and—hopefully—stop battling these illnesses.

We had dealt with a bat and needed rabies vaccines, and now we had an obvious mold problem. I was determined to explore all the possibilities, because exposure to these types of substances seemed to be seriously affecting Jack's health. But all of this raised a new question in my mind.

What other forms of toxicity were we dealing with?

The Toxic Burden of the Modern World

I love technology and all the benefits of modern living. But industrialization and technological developments create products and by-products that pollute our planet. Unfortunately, we are exposed to many of these on a daily basis.

Wireless devices, for example, are extremely convenient. But we are surrounded by the electromagnetic radiation they emit, and it disrupts the blood-brain barrier that protects a child's developing brain. Old houses can hide well-known toxins such as asbestos and lead paint. Even new building materials can be hazardous—they can emit volatile organic compounds (VOCs), and the treated wood used in their construction can contain arsenic. The Environmental Protection Agency notes that VOCs are gases that "may have short- and long-term adverse health effects."

Pharmaceuticals can make their way into our water supply. I was shocked when a colleague discovered some serious heart medications, among other things, in a sample of tap water. While the parts per million (ppm) might be minuscule, the cumulative effect these substances have on our biology warrants serious consideration.

The Environmental Working Group (EWG), a consumer watchdog organization for environmental and personal health, published a landmark study in 2005 titled "Body Burden: The Pollution in Newborns." This report is nothing short of eye opening. The Red Cross randomly tested the umbilical cord blood of newborn babies born in the United States in 2004. Tests revealed 287 chemicals in the group, including pesticides; consumer product ingredients; and wastes from burning coal, gasoline, and garbage. Of the 287 chemicals detected, 180 are known to cause cancer, 217 are toxic to the brain and nervous system, and 208 were shown to cause birth defects and abnormal development in animal testing.

Every single one of the babies had over 209 of the listed chemicals in their umbilical cord blood. That is on day one of their little lives—the blood that is circulating in their veins before they have even taken their first breath is already tainted. Children born today are swimming in toxicity! Now add to that "body burden" a daily dose of chemicals from food, personal-care products, household cleaning products, furniture, carpets, and the air, and the logic sets in.

The World Health Organization's website on children's environmental health had this to say about outdoor air pollution:

> Outdoor air pollution is large and increasing as a consequence of the inefficient combustion of fuels for transport, power generation and other human activities like home heating and cooking. Combustion processes produce a complex mixture of pollutants that comprises of both primary emissions, such as diesel soot particles and

lead, and the products of atmospheric transformation, such as ozone and sulfate particles.

Urban outdoor air pollution is estimated to cause 1.3 million deaths worldwide per year. Children are particularly at risk due to the immaturity of their respiratory organ systems.

As if pollution in the air we breathe is not enough to worry about, our tap water, which is regulated by state governments, contains "acceptable" levels of many chemicals. In October 2013, EWG reported on California's proposal of a drinking water standard for the cancer-causing substance known as hexavalent chromium. Opponents of the standard said that the state's maximum contaminant level of 10 parts per billion (ppb) was way too high. They argued that besides the known carcinogenic effects of hexavalent chromium, the state's own public health officials have highlighted other potential health risks, such as liver toxicity at levels below the proposed standard. But because of cost-benefit calculations for the proposed 10 ppb standard, the department approved it in 2014.

Our food supply is another potential problem for toxicity, especially as it pertains to genetically modified organisms (GMOs). The purpose of genetically modifying crops like corn and soybeans is to allow for disease resistance and increase the yield. Corn and soybeans are the largest GMO crops in the United States, and it is estimated that 60 to 70 percent of the processed food in our grocery stores contains GMOs.

So why is genetic modification of food even a problem? In 2009, the American Academy of Environmental Medicine (AAEM) stated, "Several animal studies indicate serious health risks associated with GM [genetically modified] food consumption including infertility, immune dysregulation, accelerated aging, dysregulation of genes associated with cholesterol synthesis, insulin regulation, cell signaling, and protein formation, and changes in the liver, kidney, spleen and gastrointestinal system." The AAEM has asked physicians to advise all patients to avoid GM foods.

Furthermore, the European Union (EU) has the strictest rules on GMOs in the world. In June 2014, and after a decade of legal battles, the EU reached an agreement allowing its member states to restrict or ban GMO crops in their territory.

Why do we care about all of these toxic influences? The health risks associated with any one of them are numerous. Toxicity in water, air, food, manufacturing, and other aspects of our environment is associated with cancer, immune system disruption, birth defects, toxicity to the brain and nervous system, liver toxicity, and more. The list goes on and on.

Is there any wonder why so many children today are being diagnosed with autism?

Toxicity in Our Environment and Autism

According to the United States Centers for Disease Control, 1 in 54 children in Utah has been identified as being on the autism spectrum. This is a number that has come close to tripling since 2002. In response to this epidemic, the Harvard School of Public Health published a study online in *Environmental Health Perspectives* in June 2013. This study sought to link autism to the exposure infants had in the womb to high levels of air pollution.

Autism is, in part, a manifestation of a poisoned planet. While I believe there is more to the big picture than simply the physical insults that we humans endure, the causes of autism can be linked to toxic or environmental exposures in predisposed children. For children who develop autism, some toxic tipping point is reached. Their biochemical pathways are broken to the point that their bodies find novel ways of functioning to cope.

There is a growing consensus in mainstream science that supports this idea that environmental causes contribute to the development of autism in a predisposed child. These environmental causes are numerous, but answers can be found in geographical clusters, as was the case with the story behind the Harvard study about Utah.

We have many theories as to who exactly is predisposed to autism, though the lines are blurring as the incidence of autism continues to explode. We know that large numbers of children with autism come from families with immune or autoimmune problems (like lupus, multiple sclerosis, rheumatoid arthritis, thyroid disease) and methylation problems (like schizophrenia and bipolar disorder). When you combine these predispositions with enough environmental toxins, autism seems almost inevitable.

The intricacies of the human body and the sheer number of possibilities for toxic exposure make it impossible to pinpoint a cause for all cases of autism. I think of it as a layering of toxicity, from the time spent in the womb and maternal body burden, to exposures in the critical early developmental years.

The authors of the Harvard study studied children from Utah as well as from all other states in the nation, all of whom were born between 1987 and 2002. They sought to correlate rates of autism to pollution levels in the areas where the mother lived while pregnant. Data showed that the children who developed autism had a statistically significant likelihood of having been exposed to high levels of air pollution while in the womb. Exposure in the womb to diesel, lead, manganese, mercury, methylene chloride, and an overall measure of metals was "significantly associated with autism spectrum disorder," with the highest association from exposure to diesel exhaust. "Air pollution," the study said, "contains many toxicants known to affect neurological function and to have effects on the fetus *in utero.*"

Another environmental link to autism can be found in a 2007 study published by researchers with the Public Health Institute. They sought to determine if there was any correlation between mothers who lived near agricultural pesticide applications and the incidence of autism among their children, theorizing that maternal residence near certain pesticides during key periods of gestation could be associated with the development of autism spectrum disorders. They looked at the application of organochlorine pesticides in quantity (poundage) and the distance of mothers from the application site. They found a significant increase in autism risk associated with the poundage of pesticide applied, and that risk decreased with increased distance from field sites.

Researchers with the University of Texas Health Science Center at San Antonio published a study in 2009 linking air pollution and autism. Specifically, they looked at the prevalence of autism in Texas school districts across all counties in 2002 and the amount of industrial mercury released from coal burning and other industrial facilities in 1998. They found a direct correlation between pounds of mercury released and increased autism rates. Furthermore, there was an inverse relationship of autism rates to distance from source, with autism prevalence diminishing 1.4 to 2 percent for every ten miles away from the industrial or power plant source.

The evidence continually adds up each year confirming the multifactorial nature of environmental exposure and autism risk. There are new and different studies that underline the same basic fact: the toxicity of our planet has in part caused the epidemic of autism we now face.

Vaccinations and Autism

Anyone who has any exposure at all to today's media is likely aware of the debate currently under way as to whether vaccinations cause autism. It is a debate that has become highly controversial and charged. Some people believe that vaccinations must be eliminated, while others believe that young children require more immunizations. It is unfortunate that the debate has created two vehemently opposed sides, because while it is possible that there is a correlation, it is not viable to stop vaccinating children.

The most helpful discussion should not be about whether to vaccinate, but how to vaccinate in a safe manner with safe vaccines.

Vaccines are intended to prompt our immune system to build antibodies against a particular virus or bacteria. They do this by exposing us to a small amount of weakened (live) or killed virus or bacteria. Our immune system then mounts a response by creating antibodies to remove it. If we come into contact with the actual virus or bacteria, our immune system is then prepared to take it out, allowing us to go unscathed, or at the very least get minimally sick.

Unfortunately, infants' bodies are not as equipped to mount the appropriate immune response as older children. Their immune systems are too immature. For example, if a child receives their first DTaP vaccine after age two, they need only two doses to be immunized. But when we start immunizing the child as an infant, they receive a total of five doses of DTaP. Today our children receive approximately 36 vaccines by age 6, which is more than triple the 10 vaccines children received in 1983.

Along with an increasingly rigorous vaccination schedule, vaccines have toxic ingredients like aluminum and formaldehyde. And the mercury that was removed from *all* childhood vaccines is still in the influenza vaccine—which is given to children *every* year.

I also have concerns about the timing of certain vaccines. For example, Hepatitis B is a disease that is only contracted by exposure to an infected person's body fluids. Certainly an infant born to an infected mother should be vaccinated. But all United States–born children are vaccinated with the hepatitis B vaccine at birth, again at 2 months old, and again at 6 to 18 months old. Yet children are not at risk for hepatitis B until they become teenagers who engage in sexual activity or use IV drugs—so why must all infants be given the vaccine? The argument is that the first year of life is an opportune time to ensure they receive the vaccine, since teenagers are harder to get to the doctor. I believe that this is a vaccine that you can choose to give on a delayed schedule, particularly if your child shows any adverse reactions to vaccines.

Another vaccine that might be delayed or omitted for many in the general population is the varicella (chicken pox) vaccine. A select few might benefit from preventing this illness, but I believe it is not necessary for healthy children. I also disagree with the new practice of giving this vaccine with the combined measles, mumps, and rubella (MMR)—four live viruses in one shot. If you do choose to vaccinate your child against chicken pox, consider keeping the varicella vaccination separate from the MMR.

It is important to remember, however, that the risk of an outbreak of most of these diseases still exists. As of the year of this writing, 2014, we have had a record number of cases of measles in the United States: 592. From 2001 to 2012, the median number of cases a year in the U.S. was 60. About 1 in 1,000 people will die from measles, so it is wise to widely immunize to prevent an outbreak. Pertussis is another disease that has resurged, and in 2013 there were over 18,000 cases in the United States. Half of infants who get pertussis need to be hospitalized, and most pertussis-related deaths are infants, so clearly it is worth vaccinating in a safe manner.

My purpose in exploring this issue is not to convince you one way or the other about the correlation between vaccinations and autism, but to incite a course of action that protects us from these infectious diseases while still also keeping our children safe from potentially harmful ingredients and regimens. Much work needs to be done in this arena, but meeting in the middle and opening the discussion will serve our children and their futures most effectively.

Relieving Your Child of the Toxic Burden

Ever since Jack's diagnosis of autism, certain things have come to my attention. Even if I originally met these topics with resistance, they have made me more conscious and aware. This is particularly true in considering the extent to which we pollute our planet and our bodies.

As we began the process of healing with Jack, we kept finding more issues to address. We discovered not just the toxic black mold but lead paint in the fireplace bricks. And these were just the tip of the iceberg. We considered chemicals in our food, water, cleaning supplies, and personal-care products. We even learned of the electromagnetic radiation coming from cordless devices and microwaves. I was surrounded by potential toxins.

As a result, I was quite frazzled in those early days. It was overwhelming and it seemed to never end. But I began with our food. I chose organic, whole foods and avoided processed and packaged foods. Then I moved on to personal care products and I discovered the Skin Deep database of the Environmental Working Group at www.ewg.org/skindeep, which is the best resource around to make the process simple.

I'm a huge fan of the EWG. They provide research on thousands of chemicals and products with the intention of informing the public about consumer safety. When you log on to their website, you can search any type of personal-care product and get the facts about toxicity. They rank products like shampoo, toothpaste, baby soap, and sunscreen from 0 to 10. The safest products are ranked 0 to 2, and as the amount of chemicals and potential toxins in the product increases, the number increases.

After researching all kinds of alternative cleaning solutions, I eliminated harsh household products and substituted natural cleaners like castile soap and white vinegar. I learned that fabric softener often contains some of the worst chemicals we can be exposed to and happily discovered that white vinegar in the fabric softener cup eliminates static cling and softens clothes. I also chose things like furniture, rugs, paint, and other household items that do not emit VOCs (volatile organic chemicals). As I discovered all kinds of effective—and cheap—alternatives, I began feeling really good about my choices. I was eliminating toxins around my home, and also cutting back on polluting the planet.

This might seem overwhelming and mysterious, but it doesn't have to be. Start small. Choose organic food when you can and eliminate any food products that have GMOs. Then you can move on to things like personal-care products. Use the EWG Skin Deep database to choose better, less toxic options. Start with shampoo, body lotion, toothpaste, makeup, and anything else you put on your and your family's bodies. Get familiar with the harmful ingredients in your personal-care products like sodium lauryl sulfate (SLS), parabens, and other chemicals. In a short time, you can become an expert at reading labels and picking out the good-for-you products.

Familiarize yourself with alternative, green cleaning products like white vinegar and castile soap. There are many books and wonderful online resources available. If you paint your house or buy new furniture, choose low odor, non-VOC products. Choose pajamas for your children that are snug fitting and are not treated with chemicals to be flame-retardant. If you buy a new mattress, get one that doesn't have flame-retardant or other harmful chemicals in it. And do not use pesticides and weed killers on your lawn or garden.

Install a simple water filter under the sink and in the shower. Drink filtered tap water instead of bottled water. If you have a damp basement, run a dehumidifier. Run a HEPA filter in bedrooms during high pollen count seasons.

There is growing research into the link between electromagnetic radiation (EMR) exposure and permeability of the blood-brain barrier. This link has been attributed to autism and ADHD as well. However, the EMR question was initially a hard one for us to address. We had a building biologist evaluate and test our home, and he had a long list of action items for us. He wanted us to get rid of all cordless phones, turn off the Wi-Fi at night, stop using the microwave, turn off the main power to my children's room at night, and many other tasks. We actually did all of these things at first, but I have made some realistic modifications since it was just not practical.

To get started, I recommend you do the three things we do for ourselves: Do away with any cordless phones. The EMR emitted from these phones is by far the biggest household exposure. Turn off the Wi-Fi at night. And keep your children from using cellular phones. All this will dramatically decrease EMR exposure.

When it comes to detoxifying the environment in which you raise your family, start small. Pick and choose what makes sense for your child and your family. When you stop the incoming exposures, the body burden can ease up and healing can occur.

When we moved from our house in Bridgehampton in March 2007, it was not easy going. We left the house the day we found out about the black mold but that wasn't the end of it. I still had to go back with a truck to get large items like my children's furniture and all of our clothes.

Jack had been getting applied behavior analysis (ABA) therapy every day in a special room we had set up for him in Bridgehampton. When we got to the new house, we had to set up a similar room, but it was challenging because there were no extra bedrooms. We converted a little den into his therapy room.

This was Jack's first move since he was born, and it seemed as though he sensed our anxiety and tension. We would be able to live in this house until the end of May, but then we had to find another house. Summer in the Hamptons was an insane rental market, so it would be challenging to find something reasonable. But the relief we felt from leaving behind the mold was also a big deal. The first night in the house, I lay with Jack and Sam as they were falling asleep. I had an overwhelming sense of calm and peace. I knew that Jack's asthma and sinus infections would stop.

I was right. Within the first month of living in the new house, Jack's health was improving. By April, he was no longer suffering from chronic sinus infections and he has never had another asthma attack.

One day I sat with Jack on the sofa in the den. We were looking out the window, and from where we were sitting I could see Pat go outside and get into his car.

"Daddy go!"

I looked at Jack, who was watching his father.

My son had just said his first two-word sentence since his diagnosis.

I could barely contain myself. I picked him up, jumped up and down, and we bounced around the room.

"Yes, Jack! Yes! Daddy go!" I said. I was thrilled at his sentence and wanted him to know how amazing he was.

One month after we left the toxicity of Bridgehampton, we had this major breakthrough. These kinds of little miracles have become common in my world today. I still jump up and down in response, and Jack and I dance around the room together.

Chapter Four

BALANCING ENERGY

Right before the holidays of 2009, I took Jack to see a homotoxicologist in New York City named Mary Coyle. She is the mother of a boy with special needs and a certified homeopath. When we arrived at her office in Manhattan, we found ourselves in a predictably tiny office, but the efficiency of how she used the space suggested that it was well thought out. A cozy white couch faced a computer system, and amidst toys and books there was an assortment of devices that looked rather futuristic.

"How are you doing, peanut butter?" she said to Jack.

Jack actually glanced up at her. I found this term unusual, but given how Jack responded, it ultimately seemed endearing.

She sat with me and explained her equipment before giving Jack a copper rod to hold. This device interfaced with her computer system. She described the process as the equipment analyzed his body systems. "We are measuring the degree of imbalance in different organ systems," she offered.

The computer program on the screen showed a line graph type of interface, recording the highs and lows of energy. I watched as the program ran through a series of spikes and valleys. She then touched a different device on dozens of different points on Jack's head, hands, and feet and recorded these readings.

"I am running through each of the body systems that can be negatively impacted by toxins," she explained. "To do this, I am measuring specific organs like the liver or kidneys by selecting their corresponding meridian points on Jack's body."

I had already researched homotoxicology, so I was up to speed with its general premise. It was developed by the German physician Hans-Heinrich Reckeweg. It is the study of the influence of homotoxins (*homo* = human being, *toxin* = poison) on the human organism. By utilizing homeopathic preparations, it attempts to detoxify the body, correct disrupted immunological processes through immunomodulation, and support cells and organs. Unlike traditional Western medicine, homotoxicology focuses on causes of disease rather than clinical symptoms.

When Mary finished gathering all of the readings, she reviewed each one with me. She wrote out very specifically which remedies we would begin with, how to take them, and what to expect.

"When children release toxins using these remedies, it's not uncommon for them to fall apart emotionally. It's very possible that Jack will experience crying spells or extreme spells of melancholy." She also described other possible reactions like increased stimming behavior and hyperactivity.

"I can hardly wait," I told Mary, half-joking. Still, I was certainly intrigued by her prediction.

We left her office and I remember how I felt that familiar optimism settle in. But this time I was approaching Jack's healing process from a holistic view. Homotoxicology sought to eliminate toxins that were blocking Jack's own innate ability to heal.

We began the remedies without a problem. For a change, they were easy enough to administer, and they didn't have an awful taste. I was happy to pack them to bring them with us on our annual trip to Maine for the Christmas festival in Kennebunkport a short while later. We had been going to Maine for a few years and this year would be no different.

Over the few years since Pat and I had gotten married, we had loved going to the Christmas shops to buy ornaments to add to our collection. It was our first little tradition together and in fact, I'd been pregnant with Jack on our first winter trip to Maine. I had just received the news that my amniocentesis was completely normal so we had cause to celebrate. Knowing the baby was going to be fine, I finally allowed myself to purchase a toy for him. I bought him a stuffed animal—a lamb—that today is a bittersweet reminder of our times in Maine and how I had hoped that I would have a completely "typical" baby.

On the trip immediately after our session with Mary, we arrived in Kennebunkport pretty late. Pat and I got the boys ready for bed right away. Jack was five and a half, Sammy was four, and Ben was eight months old. We rented a house and the boys' bedroom had a bunk bed. The bottom bunk was a full-size bed so I put the older boys together and settled Ben into the portable crib.

I lay down with them so they would feel comfortable falling asleep in this unfamiliar house. Ben and Sam fell asleep immediately, but Jack did not. I lay with him and stared up at the wooden slats of the top bunk and thought the boys would love this setup in the morning. It was like being in a fort. But Jack was pretty restless, and soon he began to whimper.

I held Jack closer. Soon his whimpers turned to sobs. For the next 30 minutes, Jack sobbed and sobbed. They were not screams, like he was in physical pain; they were just sad, drawn-out sobs. How could a five-year-old boy hold that much pain inside?

Finally, he fell asleep. I was somewhat freaked out by this display of emotion, but in a way, I was also relieved. Mary Coyle had predicted crying spells and extreme melancholy as Jack rid himself of the toxins in his body.

And that was exactly what had come to pass.

Creating a Shift in the Body

It was not long ago that most of us born in the West did not know what acupuncture or herbal medicine were. But today, what we know as alternative medicine is becoming much more accepted and understood. A large number of medical schools began embracing complementary and alternative medicine (CAM) as a viable course of study around 1999. They began implementing this type of curriculum, also known as integrative or mind-body medicine, into their training programs.

Although opinions about CAM are heated, there is no question that patients use it. The Centers for Disease Control and Prevention released data in 2008 that nearly 40 percent of adults and 12 percent of children use at least one alternative therapy. Unfortunately, many doctors are ignorant of the most up-to-date research on alternative therapies, which causes them to be reluctant to consider any for the treatment of autism. By maintaining the old way of thinking, they possibly miss an opportunity to prescribe something that could help the patient. Then, when the patient has exhausted all conventional treatments, they pursue alternative therapies on their own.

That was the path that I followed during the early days of Jack's diagnosis. I went to Mary Coyle a good two years after having tried many biomedical approaches. But lack of knowledge of these therapies does not negate the powerful effects they can have.

Many of the therapies that can be very beneficial for autism fall under the umbrella of energy work, or energy healing. Broadly described, these are therapies that manipulate or shift energy to elicit the body's own innate healing response to a substance or provocation. Some of these therapies have been around for thousands of years, but the evolution of conventional medicine has led to the exclusion of such therapies in favor of new drug discoveries and more modern approaches to medicine. These other therapies then share the title of being an "alternative" to those we have embraced in the mainstream.

This realm of modalities might seem bogus to many because the healing that occurs is often subtle. What we manipulate in these systems (e.g., energy meridians in acupuncture) is invisible or not easily definable in a laboratory. When we examine one technique, like the needles in acupuncture, and compare it to another technique, like taking pills, the processes may seem vastly different. And in many ways, they are. However, not only can the end goal be considered similar (eliminating a symptom), the two approaches share a more meaningful commonality: a precise mechanism of action that has a distinct effect on the body and mind.

There is much scientific evidence that shows how the mechanisms of action of alternative therapies are quite effective. One of my favorite scientific studies that does this was done in the 1980s by two French researchers, Drs. Jean-Claude Darras and Pierre De Vernejoul. These two researchers sought to confirm that acupuncture meridians (the pathways through which the body's vital energy, or chi, flows) do exist. They injected radioactive technetium into the acupoints of patients and used nuclear scanning to follow the flow of the technetium. They also injected non-acupoints as a control.

At non-acupoints, the radioactive tracer diffused outward from the injection site. When the true acupoints were injected, the radioactive tracer followed the exact pathways of the acupuncture meridians. Furthermore, when a needle was inserted along a meridian, the radioactive tracer downstream of the needle changed flow rate, thus confirming the stimulation of vital energy by acupuncture needles.

Alternative therapies can prove substantially effective for many common maladies, such as insomnia or anxiety, because taking a whole-body balancing approach can eliminate not just symptoms but their underlying cause. I also believe that all diseases have an emotional component, and that this is as important as the more definable physical component. In other words, we cannot separate the body's organ systems from the emotional and spiritual makeup of the person.

When we consider the intricate nature of imbalances in a child with autism, then a whole-body, energy-shifting approach makes good sense. Focusing on a single organ system might help to some degree, but a lasting return to health is far more likely to stem from a more holistic approach.

The following are my three favorite holistic modalities that I have found extremely beneficial to my son and for difficult-to-treat symptoms of autism. While each therapy adds to the body's own ability to heal by enacting different mechanisms, you can use them together to restore balance overall. And while the different modalities embrace varying frameworks for creating a shift in the body and mind, they all have a similar goal: to restore the balance of the child holistically.

Homeopathy

Open though I was to unconventional treatments, I was still skeptical when I entered into Mary Coyle's office with Jack. So many other therapies had promised so much, but were still a disappointment! But when Jack reacted with such emotional release on that night in Maine, I became a believer—solid and convinced.

Homotoxicology is just one branch of the bigger field of homeopathy. Homeopathy was developed in 1796 by the German doctor Samuel Hahnemann. It exerts its effects on the human body by eliciting a natural healing response to a substance that would, if given in high doses, actually cause the same symptoms the patient is trying to cure. This is in contrast to Western medicine's approach of providing a drug that directly exerts an effect on a specific biological process.

In this way, homeopathy is based on the premise that like cures like. A substance that causes symptoms of disease in a healthy person will cure these symptoms in a sick person. For example, when you cut an onion, your eyes will likely water. A homeopathic remedy for symptoms of itchy, watery eyes is made up of onion extract. The symptoms can be eliminated by using a substance that causes a similar reaction in a healthy person.

The remedies, made up of substances from a plant (like an onion), a mineral, or an animal, are prepared by repeatedly diluting the substance in alcohol or water. Dilution usually continues to the point that no molecules of the original substance remain—only its energetic imprint. As you can probably imagine, this is where the great controversy comes in. How can a substance that only *energetically* remains in the water have an impact on anything—and more specifically, heal the body?

The scientific community is hard pressed to accept anything it cannot see, and using an energetic imprint as medicine certainly qualifies as quackery to some. But when one very skeptical scientist set out to debunk homeopathy as scientifically implausible, she received a bit of a surprise.

Madeleine Ennis, a pharmacologist and asthma researcher at Queen's University in Belfast, sought to disprove the theory that a chemical remedy diluted to the point that it no longer contained a single molecule of anything except water could still have a healing effect. Her research findings were published in the journal *Inflammation Research* in 2004. Ennis and her team looked at the effects of highly diluted solutions of histamine on human white blood cells involved in inflammation. The study, which took place in four different labs, found that homeopathic solutions—so dilute that the probability of the solution containing a single histamine molecule was near zero—actually worked just like histamine. Ennis admitted it was totally unexpected but clearly warranted further investigation.

Homeopathy can be particularly powerful in autism as it is a modality that treats the whole person. And given how autism is complicated in both physical and emotional realms, the holistic nature of homeopathy can address the child's needs on many levels.

There are a number of examples of how it addresses more than just individual symptoms or systems. Classical homeopathy is the founding discipline that is based on the "like cures like" principles mentioned above. It is best used for relieving acute symptoms of any common malady like a cold, stomach flu, or hay fever. But, in the hands of an excellent homeopathic practitioner, it can also be used to provoke very deep healing.

Sequential homeopathy is based on a timeline of traumas, physical and emotional, that are addressed from the most recent back to birth. This process even goes back to ancestral issues that may be carried on in current generations. It is based on the energetic imprint of an event and the use of a homeopathic preparation to shift the blocked energy in a person by systematically addressing any trauma that is stuck within the energy field. Rudi Verspoor at the Hahnemann Center for Heilkunst in Canada is an excellent practitioner for addressing healing from this perspective.

CEASE Therapy (Complete Elimination of Autistic Spectrum Expression) was developed by Dr. Tinus Smits on the hypothesis that autism is caused by an accumulation of stress and toxic factors. These factors might be antibiotics, vaccines, or childhood infections like strep throat or Epstein-Barr virus. They are individually addressed by giving the child a homeopathic remedy for the specific factor. As all of the stresses or toxic factors are addressed, the child is able to return to a state of balance. Parents that have seen a noticeable decline in their child after a specific event, whether it is a vaccine or an illness, may find CEASE therapy to be a powerful healing modality.

Homotoxicology, the method used with Jack at the beginning of this chapter, is a homeopathic practice of ridding the body of toxins that may be contributing to disease. It looks specifically at organ systems and potential toxic buildup and sets out to provide remedies that will provoke the drainage and elimination of these toxins and allow the body to restore itself to balance. Overall, the effect is similar to CEASE therapy. But it more broadly looks at organ systems and body function instead of homing in on specific incidents like vaccines or bacterial infections.

But regardless of which system is used and where it is practiced, the mechanism of action of all of these forms of homeopathy is the same: a highly diluted substance is chosen to provoke the body's own healing response. I tell parents that the decision to choose one method over another is largely based on what the parent believes might have been an influencing factor in their child's autism. But another factor is the availability of practitioners. Some parents feel strongly about seeing a "well-known" practitioner, like Mary Coyle, and will travel long distances to see her. Others cannot make the trip or would be better served to find a homotoxicologist or CEASE therapist in their own neighborhood with whom to build a long-term relationship. Much goes into choosing the correct remedy, and a trial-and-error approach is necessary for some children. In my own practice, a little boy showed vast improvement in his symptoms with a combination of diet, supplements, and homotoxicology. Even Jack had a significant emotional release through the sobbing that Mary Coyle had predicted.

Each of these practitioners has shared remarkable stories with me. A classical homeopath in New York City described to me a phenomenal story of a little boy whose symptoms related to autism completely resolved with a single remedy, termed the *similium*. He described the similium as the substance with pathogenic symptoms most closely resembling the disease in the patient. The homeopath explained that it is very rare to have such a profound effect with one remedy; as we've discussed, there is unlikely to be a silver-bullet remedy for any one child. However, as was the case for this little boy, sometimes the stars all align.

Acupuncture

Most of us have either experienced the benefits of acupuncture firsthand or know someone who has. It is perhaps one of the most accepted alternative therapies available in the West and is even covered by some health insurance companies. I am really excited about its general acceptance, because I believe it can help children with autism a great deal.

Acupuncture was developed over 2,000 years ago in China. At its core, it is a process that corrects imbalances in the flow of energy in the body, called *chi* or *qi*. This energy is often referred to as the life force energy, and it plays a role in most of the ancient cultures. In China, it is called *chi*; in India, *prana*; in Japan, *ki*; and for Native Americans, it is called the *Great Spirit*. The idea of life force is central to many cultures' healing modalities.

A strong life force makes a human being thrive in vibrant wellness, while a weak force results in sluggishness, fatigue, and illness. Acupuncture is based on balancing and enhancing chi to bring the body into a state of health. This is achieved by placing tiny needles (or using pressure stimulators or lasers) along energy meridians, which are the pathways for the flow of chi.

There have been many studies done in the West to validate acupuncture, including the largest one done by doctors at Memorial Sloan-Kettering Cancer Center in New York. They published results of a meta-analysis (a review of many independent research studies) of the use of acupuncture in chronic pain in nearly 18,000 patients. The study compared the amount of chronic pain in patients who received true acupuncture treatment, sham treatments (treatments that include the use of needles but without proper placement in relation to the meridian system), and no treatment at all. The study demonstrated that patients who received true acupuncture experienced less pain than those who either received sham treatments or no treatments at all. These findings were published in October 2012 in the *Archives of Internal Medicine*, and the conclusion was that acupuncture is effective for treating chronic pain and is a "reasonable referral option." That's big news and strongly indicative of acupuncture's effectiveness.

One arm of acupuncture that I especially like for autism is called Nambudripad's Allergy Elimination Techniques (NAET), named after the physician who developed it. I find it to be a good fit for autism because it uses a pressure stimulator on the meridians instead of needles. And when treating most children, avoiding needles is a no-brainer! There are other branches of acupuncture that also do not use needles, and with a little bit of research you can likely find some other options as well.

I worked out of the office of an NAET acupuncturist for a short time when I had my private practice. His results with children with autism were incredible. I remember one little girl who had severe sensory integration problems. She could not go out in public without having a complete meltdown. She would scream, throw herself on the floor, cover her ears, and wail. Any level of noise was just too much for her.

When I saw this little girl in the acupuncturist's office after she had received treatment, she exhibited behaviors that suggested that this issue was no longer a problem. She moved freely about the room without covering her ears, and she remained calm throughout my entire interaction with her. She no longer had meltdowns and was able to go out in public on a regular basis. The quality of life for her and her family was forever changed.

When acupuncture is administered, the child's system is balanced in a way that provokes a cascade of healing. For example, NAET focuses on eliminating allergies by modulating the immune system. Remember how tightly coupled the immune, digestive, and nervous systems are? When you promote balance in the immune system through acupuncture, the downstream effects are widespread. That is why the little girl with severe sensory integration problems was brought back into a state of balance.

Acupuncture has had such a meaningful impact on so many children with autism because it approaches healing from a broader perspective.

Neurofeedback

When I first learned about neurofeedback, I took Jack to see a practitioner who had a special interest in children with autism. He saw hundreds of children and had great results with many. He talked openly to me since I am a physician, sharing stories of children who improved dramatically in his practice. He told me of one child who suffered from debilitating seizures several times a day, but then improved to the point that the seizures happened less than once every few months. He also told me about a child who initially was able to speak only a few infrequent words, but after 40 sessions started speaking in full sentences.

Neurofeedback is a way of controlling one's brain waves, which control input and output functions. A healthy brain is able to do things like understand and develop language at a typical rate; it receives input in the form of a new word and is then able to synthesize this input and express output in the form of speaking and using the new word. This essential process can be considered a healthy regulated brain state. Developmental disorders, however, cause disruption of early life experience, which interferes with the child's ability to self-regulate these brain states. There are core deficits in their ability to calm physically and emotionally and to manage sensory input.

At its core, neurofeedback training teaches children to control their brain waves by providing constant feedback from a computer screen about the nature and strength of the brain waves at any given moment. If the child's brain is overaroused, it is not able to learn. Neurofeedback teaches the brain to observe and then regulate its activity, thus learning to calm itself down. By regulating arousal, this process provides the balance the brain needs to get to the work of learning.

From a brain perspective, neurofeedback addresses two major aspects of autism: the state of overarousal of the brain and the underdeveloped functional connectivity of the neural networks that connect different parts of the brain. Furthermore, the underdeveloped connections between different parts of the brain are trained to fire together using neurofeedback. This process of *firing* together causes *wiring* together. In other words, brain plasticity is stimulated and more robust wiring enhances connectivity of different parts of the brain.

In autism, the overaroused brain can be seen in symptoms such as hyperactivity, anxiety, rapid heart rate, and extreme hypersensitivity to sensory input. The underdeveloped connections between different parts of the brain can be seen as the inability to develop language and speech and the inability to follow typical social development.

The process of neurofeedback is very simple. Sensors are attached to the head and the child sits facing a computer screen where various video games or other interfaces are shown to the child. I use a movie interface so my family can watch a movie while undergoing neurofeedback. The child's own electrical activity in their brain controls the images, changing what happens on the screen. The brain is able to recognize its ability to control the images—hence the *feedback*. This loop is observed and reinforced hundreds of times during a session.

Neurofeedback allows a child's own brain to learn core regulation. The child with the seizures experienced the symptoms that he did because he had totally dysregulated brain waves. As a result of the sessions he underwent, he was able to retrain his brain to stabilize and reduce the reactivity of various input functions. In turn, he experienced better brain function and had fewer seizures as a result.

Making the Most of Alternative Therapies

A child with autism is such a unique, sensitive, and brilliant individual. They are the epitome of individuals who benefit from a holistic approach. I had this inkling that because of the extent of his physiological imbalances, Jack wouldn't be able to heal with biomedical approaches alone.

As you've seen, there are many different forms of alternative therapy. And as you've also seen, there are even many different approaches and mind-sets within one form, like with homeopathy. But the qualities they all share are also their most powerful asset: They all seek to balance energy and allow the body's innate healing response to kick in. And, they are extremely safe.

You may want to consider Reiki, a "laying on of hands" healing approach that allows the life-force energy to flow and restore balance in the body. A similar technique, Pranic healing, is an energy flowing/unblocking discipline that seeks to balance prana. I have several friends who are Reiki masters, and I took several courses in Pranic healing and really enjoyed the meditative component, the setting of intentions, and the coursework on the major and minor chakras—the energy centers in the body that both transmit and receive energy.

I also love to use essential oils. Each oil has a certain frequency and can be used for specific applications. Lavender is widely used in the West for its calming properties; you may have noticed that lavender is added to many bedtime or nighttime products like baby washes, soaps, and lotions.

There are entire books on energy healing modalities. Laser light healing and detoxification, footbaths, infrared saunas, Qigong, and the list goes on. I have found my big three to be very powerful and accessible, and these other techniques are all worth exploring as they arise on your path.

Because each child with autism is unique, the healing process you choose will be to some degree trial and error as is the process outlined in Chapter 2. Not everything works for everyone, but there are some larger guideposts that can point you in the right direction. And the very best place to receive ongoing guidance is to work with a compassionate practitioner who has a special interest in children with autism. Your instincts are the most important factor in this process, so choose systems that feel right for you and your family.

When I educate practitioners and parents about the best approach for their particular child, I always start with the question: What are the three biggest issues that you would like to address? From there, I ask about three lesser issues that are troublesome.

There are common issues that children with autism share, but only the parent can say to what degree each dominates. Modalities can be chosen based on the predominant issues. The following list of symptoms are common to children with autism, and for each one I've provided general guidelines that may be beneficial to them:

- If your child has allergies, asthma, and/or eczema, he will likely benefit from acupuncture.

- If your child is thin and does not gain weight, he will likely benefit from acupuncture.

- If your child has self-injurious behavior, he will likely benefit from neurofeedback.

- If your child has seizures, he will likely benefit from neurofeedback.

- If your child is nonverbal and very hyperactive, he will likely benefit from neurofeedback, but if your child is nonverbal and extremely allergic, he might benefit from acupuncture first.

- If your child is hyperactive and does not sleep, he will likely benefit from homeopathy and then neurofeedback once he becomes calmer.

- If your child is always stimming, he will likely benefit from homeopathy.

There really is no successful cookie-cutter way to approach a child with autism. The variables serve as clues to help us determine which approach to start with. A highly stimming child with severe eczema would not necessarily start at the same place as a highly stimming child with seizures. But the beauty of all of these alternative modalities is their safety profile.

In opening up to the world of energy work, I have uncovered possibilities that otherwise might never have taken place. I have been initiated into the emotional and spiritual realms that my son's condition has demanded I take notice of. If we want to connect with our children and allow them to step into their own brilliance, then it is something we must consider.

And what an amazing journey it has been. As the science catches up to these energy healing modalities, they will become more fully embraced in the mainstream. But we don't have another hundred years. Our children, in all of their complicated brilliance, are demanding a holistic approach. Stay open and I promise you, with the right attitude and with some of these healing modalities, you will unlock possibilities for your child that you never dreamed were possible.

When I think about Jack's sobbing episode in Maine, I smile. As I began the protocol, Mary Coyle explained to me in detail that Jack might experience crying spells or periods of melancholy. I got to witness the power of homeopathy exactly as she had predicted.

But why did Jack respond as he did? He was five. He did not have any reason, from a Western point of view, to sob so intensely. He was not physically hurt or hungry, no one took away a favorite toy, his mother was with him, and he was warm and comfortable. In fact, in the hours and minutes leading up to the sobbing episode, he was quite himself.

Homeopathy works on the emotional and spiritual body of the child, not just the physical. Jack's episode was my proof that something had shifted. He released something and energy moved.

For this Western-trained physician, it was a terrific lesson in alternative therapy. All matter is defined by the constant movement of atoms and is made up of invisible, swirling protons and electrons. And yet, we see solid things like a chair or a book or a hand. The effect of a therapy isn't negated just because we don't always know its mechanism or see some proof under the microscope with our physical senses.

Since Jack's first two-word sentence of "Daddy go!" months earlier, his language sort of plateaued. He would have occasional two-word sentences, but they were few and far between. But after Maine, that all changed.

In the couple of months that followed the episode in Maine, Jack began using two-word and then *three*-word sentences on a regular basis. My husband always said it was like a light switch was turned on. I laugh to myself because it was exactly like that.

Energy flowed, and his language was our light.

Chapter Five

THE BEHAVIORAL ROAD MAP

Not long after Jack was diagnosed with autism, I tried to maintain some level of normalcy with him. I signed us up for a Mommy and Me Music Together group that met once a week in the Southampton Youth Center.

The youth center was a big sports complex for both indoor and outdoor events and our class was held in a large room in the back. The room seemed as though it was designed for ballet, because one wall was entirely made up of mirrors and a long ballet bar ran the length of the room. There were large bags and boxes of instruments and other items for making music.

All of the moms and their toddlers assembled in a circle when the instructor began the class. There were usually about 15 to 20 pairs of us, each mother sitting with her toddler in her lap as the instructor handed out instruments. One day, she handed out maracas, wooden sticks with ridges, tambourines, triangles, and other noisemakers to the children, and then had us pass them to the next mommy and toddler in a continual rotation.

The children shook the maracas and danced around. Some banged on tambourines and triangles, obviously proud of their musical abilities. They sang, smiled, and had a ball. It was a cacophony of toddler joy.

Near the end of the class, the instructor brought out a collection of beautiful drums. There were drums from all over the world and of every size. Their colorful designs and exquisite craftsmanship reminded me of exotic locations. The instructor set up a station with each of the drums and handed each of the mommies a pair of drumsticks to share with her toddler. It was the highlight of the class.

The children ran around to each of the drum stations with their sticks. They banged a little at each station, sometimes putting the sticks aside to participate in the group drumming, where children gathered at the biggest drum and added their own version of hand patter and bongo techniques.

But when the instructor handed me the drumsticks, I remember thinking, *Well, we won't be needing these.* And sure enough, while the other kids were banging on drums, my little guy was off in the corner of the room. He had intentionally positioned himself in front of the large mirror and rather than beat on his chosen drum, he spun it. He checked its position carefully, whirled it around, and checked its position again. His eyes widened and he squeaked or hummed as the drum spun perfectly and to his liking. He was totally engrossed.

He had been spinning objects like this since his slip into autism. His first and favorite spinning object was a large green plastic dog bowl that belonged to our golden retriever Jake. It was his favorite activity, and the behavior that suggested to Pat and me that something was amiss in our little boy.

Whenever I took Jack out of the house, he would find some object—no matter where we went—and spin it. He would find things on shelves of grocery stores or at the public library, for example, and spin his little heart out. People would stare. Boy, would they stare. And then they'd shoot me an apologetic look, uncomfortable with the realization that something was not normal about Jack and perhaps their reaction felt a little rude.

So as I sat in the music class and watched my boy spin the drums, a familiar feeling came up. I started to feel nervous and embarrassed, somehow figuring I was responsible for Jack's aberrant behavior. My family knew it was not my fault, and I was therefore becoming more comfortable with them. But it was much harder in public, when strangers did not know Jack had autism. It always added to my desire to find a cure—to "fix" Jack.

I looked up from Jack and noticed one of the other moms staring at him. She turned and looked at me with that uncomfortable, then apologetic expression, somehow catching herself for being a little bit rude. I did what I always did: I ran over to Jack and tried to explain the correct way to use a drum. It was the least I could do to ease the tension between her and me.

This was my reaction to Jack. I tried to "save face," as if my controlling his behavior made me a better parent. If someone didn't like what Jack was doing, it was my job to jump right in and stop the behavior.

That was what I believed for a long time. That was then.

Is Autism a Behavioral Disorder?

The American Psychiatric Association (APA) leads Western medicine in defining behavioral disorders. They publish the *Diagnostic and Statistical Manual of Mental Disorders* (now on its fifth edition, known as the DSM-5). This manual seeks to provide a standard set of criteria for the classification of mental disorders. They define mental disorders as "a behavioral or psychological syndrome or pattern that occurs in an individual."

To further clarify, behavioral disorders are considered emotional disorders with either behaviors that are expressed through outward action (like aggression, impulsivity, coercion, and noncompliance) or behaviors that are expressed inwardly, to oneself (like withdrawal, isolation, depression, and anxiety).

An example of a behavioral disorder is post-traumatic stress disorder (PTSD). It can occur following an extreme emotional trauma that involved the threat of injury or death. Some events that can lead to PTSD include military combat, terrorist incidents, physical or sexual assault in adult or childhood, a serious accident, or a natural disaster. Individuals with PTSD may exhibit avoidance behaviors like staying away from certain places, events, or objects that remind them of the traumatizing event. They may have hyperarousal symptoms that cause them to be easily startled, experience difficulty falling asleep, or have angry outbursts. Because of these symptoms, the APA considers this psychiatric condition a behavioral disorder.

Other mental disorders as defined by a set of behavioral patterns include conduct disorder, oppositional defiant disorder, bipolar disorder, and schizophrenia. A person with one of these afflictions exhibits aberrant behaviors that demonstrate a stark contrast to the behaviors of "typical" individuals.

A child with autism will exhibit aberrant behaviors as well. Some children can be seen flapping their hands excessively, while others walk around on their toes on a frequent and consistent basis. Some children may only look out of the corner of their eye. And others, like my Jack, may be seen continually spinning objects.

As we have explored throughout this book thus far, when we consider a child with autism through a biological lens, we see a nervous system that has experienced significant damage. These children's senses are often so sensitive that coping with the day-to-day input to their brain becomes overwhelming. Their immune systems are often greatly compromised, either overreacting in some cases or failing to respond appropriately in others.

A child who peers out of the corner of his eyes could be doing so because his peripheral vision is off or direct light is extremely painful to him. A child might be hand flapping because this is his only way of knowing where his arms are in space; without the flapping, he may not realize he has arms attached to his body.

These children are plagued with broken biochemistry that makes living in their own skin at best uncomfortable and at worst unbearable. And yet the APA has classified autism as a *behavioral* disorder.

The causes of the behaviors of children with autism are much different than the causes in other conditions labeled as behavior disorders like PTSD. The emotional trauma that a PTSD survivor experiences causes a pattern of behaviors as defined by the disorder. There is a direct causal relationship between the behaviors they exhibit and the event that injured them. There is no such relationship in children with autism to some specific emotional event. Their behaviors, while certainly seen as "patterns of behavior" among this group, are manifestations of them trying to survive in a body that is at best uncomfortable.

Why does this type of label even exist? There is a need in our medical model to assign a label to each pathology, and the label of autism centers on the aberrant behaviors exhibited by those with this condition. It is understandable why there is a need for a label—so the government or health insurance companies can pay for services—but, as is the case with some of the more forceful therapies, the treatment and services geared toward helping these children become driven by the desire to "correct" these behaviors.

Children with autism have a biological basis for doing what they are doing in response to well-defined disruptions of biochemistry. What good does stomping out an aberrant behavior do if we've never discovered the underlying reason for that behavior?

Because autism is seen as a behavioral disorder, the main therapy that is funded by the government and health-insurance companies is applied behavior analysis (ABA). And, as I've mentioned, the only two FDA-approved drugs for the treatment of autism are both antipsychotic drugs, which are designed to suppress undesirable behavior. We do not serve children with autism when we label them in this way. If we instead tried to understand the motivations behind their behaviors and the reasons they behave the way they do, we would better serve their needs.

Most parents want their children to fully discover their individuality, and to help them to fully realize whatever makes them special. But stomping out behaviors and trying to force conformity does the opposite.

Why Children with Autism Act as They Do

When Jack suddenly went from a typical toddler to a child insistent on spinning every object he could get his hands on, it was not in response to some traumatic emotional challenge to which he suddenly succumbed. His nervous system was injured. Plain and simple.

The human nervous system is a fascinating but delicate network of interrelated systems that creates our experience as we physically interact with our world. It is the CEO of our body, the captain of the ship. And it is what regulates everything from our senses to our heart rate to our breathing.

The central nervous system is made up of the brain and spinal cord. It is composed of a network of cells called neurons that transmit electrical signals. Our spinal cord receives information from our skin, joints, and muscles, and it carries the nerves that control our movements. Our brain receives information directly from our eyes, ears, nose, mouth, and the rest of our body via the spinal cord.

The peripheral nervous system comprises everything beyond the brain and spinal cord and it is under both voluntary and involuntary control. The voluntary part allows us to move our arms and legs via nerves from our brain to your limbs. The involuntary part is called the autonomic nervous system and it regulates things like temperature control and digestion.

The autonomic nervous system has three parts: (1) the sympathetic system, which controls the fight-or-flight response; (2)

the parasympathetic system, which controls the rest-and-digest response; and (3) the enteric system, which controls the workings of our gut.

We must understand the nervous system if we want to understand why our children behave in certain ways. There are many points of injury in this system and the complexity of the interrelatedness can manifest in any of the behaviors that are seen in our children. Because of the faulty nature of their nervous systems, children with autism can be stuck living in an overstimulating world. For many, their nervous systems are in overdrive and the fight-or-flight arm (the sympathetic arm) causes all kinds of havoc to their reality. Every child with autism is behaving in a way that mitigates the discomfort that he feels as a result of this faulty, injured wiring.

Toe walking is an example of a behavior that is easy to correlate to nervous system impairment. This behavior could be a result of a faulty vestibular system, which is a sensory system that is often impaired in children with autism. It is responsible for balance and a sense of spatial orientation. The brain receives information from the eyes, muscles, and joints, and the vestibular apparatus in the ears. It provides the leading information about movement and balance. But the toe walking could also result from a faulty visual-vestibular system, in which the child's field of vision is distorted.

No matter which area of the vestibular system is off, the child who toe walks is compensating for dysfunctional sensory processing and is trying to cope with a distorted view of his environment.

Hand flapping is also considered to be a strong sign of sensory imbalance. Some children flap their hands near their eyes, using their peripheral vision as part of the circuit, which is a strong indicator that visual input is impaired at this level. It could also be a behavior to help the child draw attention to the spatial orientation of his limbs. In other words, flapping the hands helps the child to know where his arms are in relation to his body and the surrounding space.

The way Jack loved to spin the drums at the music class was a coping mechanism that represented a child so off balance that the possibility of "normal" behavior was out of reach. Like all children who go from being typical toddlers to getting a diagnosis of autism, his nervous system had been disturbed to the point that typical was no longer possible.

What is really interesting about children labeled with autism is that, while they represent a population with particularly diverse needs, there is a striking similarity in the behaviors and characteristics that predominate in the disorder. A few of these are:

- Toe walking

- Hand flapping

- Lining up toys/objects

- Spinning objects or spinning themselves (twirling around the room)

- Delayed speech or nonverbal interaction

- Covering ears in response to many sounds

- Avoiding eye contact

- Using toys inappropriately (e.g., spinning wheels on a toy car)

- Hurting self by head banging or hand biting

- Looking out of the corner of their eyes (especially common while running along the perimeter of a property with a fence)

- Appearing deaf in that they show no startle response to loud noises

- Appearing insensitive to painful stimuli such as bruises, cuts, and injuries

- Squinting or covering eyes around different light sources
- Tasting and smelling inedible objects in the environment

I could put a list of 50 items on the page that are common behaviors seen in children with autism and can be found on any autism behavior screening checklist. The more severely the child ranks on the spectrum, the more common behaviors he seems likely to exhibit.

When Jack was first diagnosed, he had 40 out of 50 of the listed behaviors. While he had many, I was grateful he did not have self-injurious behavior like head banging, aversion to touch, or difficulties with toilet training. He has always allowed me to hold him and readily seeks out my attention when he is ready to go to bed. He likes to cuddle. He was also toilet trained by the time he was three and a half years old.

There is close to an infinite number of possible behavior combinations. Children in my private practice ranged from mild to severe on the autism spectrum and no two were alike. I can even think of equally, severely affected children with completely different presentations.

One beautiful five-year-old girl had no language but was constantly in motion. She spent much of the time whirling herself around the room, and she often lunged and darted from here to there. All the while, she flapped her hands, vocally chirped, and grunted. A little boy, also five years old and nonverbal, was very content to hold his toys and objects close to him. He would hold them up to the light, smell them, and taste them. He would keep himself totally encapsulated, neatly and predictably, in his own little environment.

One of these children flitted about the room endlessly, while the other was in total control of a small area of the room. Both were severely affected, but they had two different ways of compensating for the aspect of their nervous system that was impaired.

No matter which of these activities a child engages in, he is at his core trying to make sense of his environment, or is responding in the best way he can to an imbalance of input and output. It is therefore very important to understand the child from his perspective. Even if we do not have the exact answer as to why a behavior is occurring, it is helpful to understand that there is an imbalance. But in many cases, we can use these behaviors to get helpful clues as to where the problem lies.

Each child, with his myriad of compensatory behaviors, is a puzzle that is worth investigating. The complexities of autism shout out for an approach that includes biomedical, energetic, and behavioral considerations.

If ever there was a condition in which one size does *not* fit all, it is within the child with autism.

How We Respond to a Child's Behaviors

I am still haunted by a recent Facebook post written by a teenage girl with autism. Her post was in response to the actions of school officials and the student body toward a nonverbal teenage boy with autism.

The scene is a high school gym during a rally. The boy, covering his ears and rocking in a corner, suddenly jumps up and runs out of the gym. His aide runs after him. And then several others run after him. They drag him back into the gym. He screams and fights, trying to escape. Several hold him, pull him, and force him back into the gym. He finally acquiesces. Defeated, he sits in a corner, covers his ears, and begins rocking back and forth again.

And the student body erupts in cheers.

They shout their kudos to the aides that returned the boy to the gym. They think they did something really good. They celebrate this triumph.

The girl with autism responds in a letter. She is heartbroken. She describes the situation from his perspective. The rally is loud and clamoring. It is extremely painful to sit and listen to the noises that are escalating. Anxiety rises. The pain increases in his head and his body. His anxiety levels continue to rise. Fear grips him. It grips him so profoundly that he feels like he will die. The anxiety and fear are so overwhelming that he cannot go on another minute. So he flees.

But they bring him back and they cheer. They do not understand his world. In moments like these, society has dictated a response to behavior that is then carried out—at all costs. Heartbreaking, indeed.

In response to this story, I would like to ask you a question. Have you ever watched a typical toddler throw a tantrum? Because toddlers are in the middle of those notorious "terrible twos," they could be fine one moment but then something triggers them. And then . . . pandemonium. You might see them in the middle of a store or some other public place. They throw themselves on the floor, kicking and screaming, and they howl like a trapped animal.

These children are responding to something in their environment. Maybe they didn't get the toy they wanted or that breakfast cereal they saw on television, or perhaps they're just hungry or tired.

Tantrums have puzzled psychologists and parenting experts for decades. Lately, the consensus seems to recommend riding it out. Experts warn that trying to stop the behavior is counterproductive, and will almost certainly lead to an escalated tantrum. They say things like "Make sure the child is safe and can't hurt herself," or "Gently remove her from the public and provide a safe outlet for her to calm down."

Parents are no longer stigmatized as they used to be for having a wild child. The judgmental comment "Can't you control your child?" is not as pervasive as it used to be. Now that the responsibility for stopping the tantrum has been removed, parents are much more empathetic toward each other when they witness them.

Tantrums are a really good example of a predicament that has puzzled parents and experts for years. But what is perhaps most significant about this issue is that it has not only puzzled parents and experts, *but they have actually embraced it as a puzzle to be solved.* Many methods to help resolve the occurrence of tantrums have been tried and failed. So new methods crop up and are tried. It's a puzzle. We try. We fail. We try again until we find an acceptable solution. And through this exploration a general directive has emerged, that we must create an environment for the child so that the symptom of the issue—the tantrum—can play out in a safe, nondestructive way.

And yet, for the boy at the gym rally, the child was forced to stay in an environment despite the intense level of suffering he endured by being there. He exhibited his own symptoms—covering his ears and rocking in a corner—but instead of giving him a safe environment in which to exist, he was coerced to conform to the acceptable behavior of being in the gym at the rally.

In instances like this, autism is not seen as a puzzle.

What if the boy in the gym was met by a person who understood that his behavior was a response to his environment? What if they reached out to him and offered him a more calming environment instead? What if people understood that he was doing the best that he could under those circumstances? What if someone showed him compassion?

The way to respond to a child with autism's aberrant behavior is not to coerce him out of those behaviors, but rather to investigate the significance of them. This requires us to see these behaviors as a puzzle, and to solve a puzzle we must find answers. Finding answers requires us to ask questions.

And there are a lot of questions to ask.

What is the child experiencing? Why is the child doing what he is doing? What is going on in the child's world? What is it about his physical body or immediate environment that is perpetuating this behavior? To find answers to these questions, as parents, teachers, and caregivers of people with autism, we must educate ourselves. We must get into the minds of as many people with autism as we can and ask questions.

Solving a puzzle like this may warrant a calling in of experts, but the best expert for a child with autism is the parent. Though practitioners skilled at some aspect of healing the body, mind, or spirit can help, parents have the greatest potential to be experts because they know the child better than anyone.

Through extensive reading and my own observations of Jack, I have come to understand autism in a way that opens up possibilities for interventions that have served my son. I look at Jack and I ask questions. If he is extremely hyperactive, I wonder about something he ate, or an environmental trigger. If he covers his ears, I realize he may be overstimulated by noises. But sometimes he covers his ears, uncovers them, and covers them again, like he is experimenting with sound. I can always read whether or not he is distressed, which of course becomes significant as to whether there is an issue needing to be resolved.

There are dozens of books written by children and adults with autism. I feel that they are the best collective resource for getting answers to the broad questions about behavior and what it is like to live in their skin. My favorites are listed in the Resources section at the back of the book to form a more complete list. Some examples are *The Reason I Jump, The Mind Tree, How Can I Talk If My Lips Don't Move?,* and *Thinking in Pictures.*

We can choose how we respond to behaviors. If a child toe walks, looks out of the corner of his eye, or flaps his hands, we do not have to stop the behavior. We can accept him where he is and take useful action to heal a sensory processing system that is damaged. If a child lines up toys or is rigid about how the morning routine is done, accept where he is today and allow him the control. Rather than stopping these behaviors, work on resolving the core issues that may reside within his physiology or some other aspect of his whole being.

If a child is head banging or exhibiting some other self-injurious behavior, do not dismiss it as a natural by-product of the diagnosis. Look for answers. Work with a qualified practitioner to figure out why the child is doing this extreme behavior. Is he in pain? Does he hate going to school because he is treated poorly? People do things for a reason. Find out the reason instead of condemning the behavior.

When you get into the heart and minds of individuals with autism and you understand what it is like to live in their skin, you can approach them with compassion and meaningful interventions.

The autism puzzle is multidimensional, and we can intervene on a physical level to help these children's bodies return to balance. But we also have an opportunity to see the bigger picture of who they truly are. And if we take steps to solve their behavioral puzzle, we can see this picture for ourselves.

After the mother stared at Jack as he spun the drum, I went over to him to explain the correct way to play with it. It was my standard way of intervening. When he was doing something bizarre, I stopped the behavior.

And though the mother had looked at me with that predictably uncomfortable, then apologetic expression, at the end of class she did something different.

She approached me.

"Wow, he is really, really good at spinning that drum," she said.

"Yes" was all I could say. I felt so uneasy.

"He is truly amazing," she added. "He has perfect control over that drum. He is very skilled."

And with that, she walked away. She was sincere.

I had never considered this perspective. I watched Jack, who was still spinning away even after the class was over. He *was* really good at spinning the drum. He *had* clearly mastered this activity. He had that drum spinning with such precision it *was* quite amazing to witness. I was struck by how different it *was* to view my child through this new lens.

Jack's desire to spin objects is indeed a puzzle, and as time goes by I continue to consider what this love of his ultimately means. But after that mother approached me that day, I looked at his face. He was perfectly content and happy. He was doing something he loved. And unlike his mother, he could not have cared less about what people thought about him. He was in his joy.

In that moment, that was all that mattered.

Chapter Six

THE INNER WORLD OF A CHILD WITH AUTISM

"Jack is in a constant state of trying to return to the ecstasy of death."

The words rattled around in my head and my stomach turned. I thought I would vomit right there at the kitchen table. I was horrified. *Why would my little boy want to experience death?* I wondered.

I had recently read Rupert Isaacson's *The Horse Boy,* a story about a family's journey across Mongolia in search of the shamans that might heal their boy with autism. I knew nothing about shamans, but I felt motivated to find one. I did some research and found Sarah, a shaman in Vermont.

I had interviewed her on the phone several weeks earlier. She was a Native American from the Choctaw tribe who had discovered her gifts of insight and vision as a young girl. Her grandmother helped her to refine these abilities and taught her many other skills. There was something about her that I trusted. She seemed authentic, kind, and true.

Jack and I arrived in Montpelier, Vermont, for our first visit with Sarah on Father's Day weekend in 2008. We rented a house about five minutes outside of town. We would have several meetings with her, the first of which would take place at her office. I thought it odd that a shaman had an office, but what was I expecting? A hut or a tepee?

When we arrived, I was relieved to see that it was more like a therapy room than an office. She had a small space in an old building, erected circa 1910. Her walls were pale blue with high ceilings and large windows along one wall, and the floor was covered by an old, worn carpet. The room was filled with feathers, claws, statues, carvings, and fragrant things to burn.

There were beautiful, handmade drums of all sizes. She told me the drums were a passion and hobby for her. She told me the rhythm of the drum allowed her to get into a trancelike state where she could access the spirit world. This is one of the ways shamans receive guidance to help others. They believe that spirit guides and energies from other realms could be called upon through shamanic rituals, and then guidance could be brought forth and shared with those seeking it.

In the corner of Sarah's office was a therapy table, much like a massage table, where she did most of her work with clients. But in Jack's case, she said it would be better to let him just move about the room. So move about he did. I was to just sit in a chair, relax, and watch.

She opened the session by trying to build rapport with Jack. She offered him intriguing objects, but nothing engaged him. She started drumming very quietly with her eyes closed. Then she chanted a beautiful melody and followed him around the room, patiently but with intention. She moved her arms around while she blew smoke from burning herbs over him. And she waved an owl feather sporadically in a rhythmic motion.

And then something happened. Jack walked over to me sitting in the chair. He crouched down and nestled his head on my abdomen and stayed there for a few moments. It was unusual for him to seek comfort like that. Sarah told me it seemed he was trying to go back into my womb. I thought that was pretty weird.

At the end of that first session in her office, she told me the real work would happen that night when Jack was asleep. She arrived at our house right around bedtime and told me she would work with him while he slept. She explained things like soul retrieval, soul mending, fragmentation, and other things that made no sense to me. She spent about two hours in Jack's room, and when I peeked in intermittently she was either humming or chanting and swirling her arms around his body.

Pat and I sat patiently at the kitchen table, though we were anxious for some answers, anything to give us hope that Jack could be helped. She emerged at about 10:30 P.M. and sat with us. She explained more about her techniques and what she hoped to accomplish. And then she dropped the bomb about Jack being in a constant state of trying to return to the ecstasy of death.

After the pit in my stomach became almost too great to bear, she went on.

"Perhaps he had a near-death experience either in the womb or around his birth?" she inquired.

I thought about his birth.

"Jack was delivered by emergency caesarean section," I told her. "His heart rate dropped dangerously low every time I had a contraction, which was a strong indicator of severe fetal distress.

"When he was delivered," I continued, "the umbilical cord was wrapped around his neck, twice. Maybe this could have been a near-death experience?"

In response, Sarah went on to describe the ecstasy part of her previous statement. She talked about a return to oneness with all and a feeling of connectedness to everything. She used words like "euphoria" and "nirvana." I guess that made it a little more tolerable.

But I still did not really understand what she was saying. I felt like something profound had been revealed to me, but I had no idea how to process it.

How We See the World

When Sarah told me Jack was trying to return to the ecstasy of death, I was pretty much living as most humans live. My reality was that which I could see, hear, taste, touch, and smell. I didn't know anything about the so-called "spirit world" and I certainly didn't like the fact that my baby was in some state of trying to return to death.

But a funny thing happened to me in the years that followed that Vermont visit. Slowly, things started popping up, like little synchronicities or proof that what the shaman told me was in fact true.

I suppose that skepticism serves us well. Otherwise, if we didn't have a filter then every snake oil salesman would prey on us. But we all know historical cases of skepticism and the impact it had on the reality of the time. Remember how the world used to be flat? Or that the Earth was at the center, and not the sun, of what we now call the solar system? These beliefs were not taken lightly.

The worldview of the 15th and 16th centuries was vehemently upheld. Galileo was accused of heresy by the church because his views opposed scripture. Columbus actually had to convince his crew that they would not fall off the end of the earth on their voyage. Beliefs, especially about reality, are subject to individual interpretation. Keeping an open mind, however, can lead to some pretty phenomenal discoveries.

So why do we all believe that the earth is round and the sun is at the center of the solar system? Because we have proof. We can see it. We have pictures. We humans live on a physical plane that, for many, is the only reality there is.

In the 1800s, surgeons used to go from the anatomy lab working on cadavers to the delivery room without washing their hands. They never washed their hands because they did not believe in germs. They couldn't see them. But the mortality rate was as high as 35 percent during childbirth. Then along came a physician named Semmelweis, whose germ theory suggested that the surgeons were contributing to the high mortality rates. He published results of hand-washing studies where the mortality rate dropped to *below 1 percent.*

Surgeons were outraged. Semmelweis's observations conflicted with the established scientific and medical opinions of the time, and his ideas were rejected by the medical community. His theory was vehemently opposed. He was committed to an asylum in 1865, and was beaten to death by guards two weeks after being committed. He was 47.

Beliefs about reality are powerful.

Did the lack of scientific proof in 1865 negate the reality of germs? Nope. So why do surgeons wash their hands today? The medical community didn't change their mind because they felt bad about what they did to Semmelweis. Surgeons wash their hands because now there is scientific proof that germs exist.

Recently, there have been some scientists who have had exceptional experiences that have provided their own form of proof. Not scientific proof, *experiential* proof. I am particularly fond of these stories, because they are about Western-trained physicians like me.

Eben Alexander is an American neurosurgeon who spent 30 years honing his scientific worldview. But in 2008, he had a near-death experience. In his *New York Times* best-selling book *Proof of Heaven,* he describes his journey beyond this world. He encountered an angelic being that guided him into the deepest realms of superphysical existence. It was here that he met, and spoke with, the Divine source of the universe itself.

Brian Weiss, an American psychiatrist, had very strong, science-based views of the world until one of his patients began recalling past-life traumas that seemed to hold the key to her recurring nightmares and anxiety attacks. His skepticism was eroded when she began to channel messages from "the space between lives," which contained remarkable revelations about Dr. Weiss's family and his dead son.

In these cases, experiential proof was so strong that scientific proof was no longer necessary. And these two physicians were staunchly rooted in science. But I believe their experiences are part of a bigger movement that is under way. It is a spiritual movement that is prompting the exploration of age-old questions that ponder the meaning of existence, God, and life after death.

We have honored the analytical mind for centuries. It has driven such glorious discoveries about the physicality of ourselves and our universe. The analytical part of our mind is housed in the left half of our brain and is the seat of not only analysis but ego, judgment, and context. In contrast, the right half of our brain is the center of intuition, creativity, and empathy.

We humans are a very left brain–oriented group. We analyze, we judge, and we put things in context. But what if we tapped into our right brain? What would happen if we didn't just analyze everything but grasped our surroundings on a more intuitive level? I believe the spirituality movement is doing this and one of my favorite advocates for this type of living is a left-brain scientist named Jill Bolte Taylor. Her story landed in my e-mail inbox just weeks after we returned from the shaman in Vermont.

Dr. Taylor, a neuroanatomist, had a large left-brain stroke when she was 37 years old. During the stroke, the left side of her brain shut down, but the right side remained untouched and fully functional. She experienced a state of euphoria that she described as "one with all that is." Her perception during the stroke was that the whole world and all the creatures in it were all part of the same field of energy.

Dr. Taylor's new reality sounded distinctly similar to the reality the shaman proposed as it related to Jack.

So these scientists offer us the possibility of a new reality. We have been served well by our healthy skepticism, but there is greater potential for our children and ourselves if we at least consider this new reality.

I have come to fully embrace these possibilities. Year after year, the evidence of things like a spirit world has mounted in favor of a bigger-picture reality that is not physically apparent.

The Power of Our Higher Selves

Sarah educated me about the rituals of shamans. In particular, she taught me about her mode of healing. She told me that while she drums, she seeks a vision for Jack's healing. And through the work she does with spirit guides, she seeks a wholeness for his soul. She explained that she uses a combination of shamanic techniques known as soul retrieval, extraction healing, and soul mending.

We all sort of have an idea about what the soul is—a nonphysical immortal essence. Soul retrieval is a process to help a person recover his soul essence after he has suffered soul loss due to trauma. Extraction healing is the removal of the spiritual aspect of an illness. And soul mending is reweaving the fabric of the soul after it has been cleaned and restored to wholeness, thus strengthening the person; this brings him stability and health. It was all very foreign to me at the time.

When Sarah chanted and drummed as Jack moved about her office, she told me she had received a vision. This happened before she made the statement about the ecstasy of death. When she worked with his soul in the sleeping hours, she received confirmation of this idea and felt that he had suffered a trauma, perhaps during the birth process.

Sarah provided the opening dialogue for a new perspective from which I could view Jack. She provided insight into the significance of Jack's relationship to his soul.

Today, there is a popular spiritual term known as the "higher self." Though many use the terms "higher self" and "soul" synonymously, they are not exactly the same thing. I think about the soul as the all-encompassing energy essence that comprises all aspects of a being. One of these aspects is the higher self. This is the part of us that exhibits and possesses all of our best and most competent qualities. It is an aspect of self that contains complete human knowledge, wisdom, and understanding.

The higher self is what we tap into when we meditate. It is a powerful resource that each of us has access to within ourselves and is the entity that can guide us toward our highest good.

I have come a long way since my initial meeting with Sarah and have engaged in an ongoing process with a number of spiritual coaches. One of them, my aligning coach, facilitates the process of aligning with the higher self. As we do this, we connect to our capacity to feel unconditional love, compassion, knowledge, and joy. We *evolve*.

She explained it like this. We interact in day-to-day life from a physical plane. It is the place where we act from our five senses. Just above the physical plane is our heart center, and above the heart center is our higher self. So it is like a hierarchy of sorts. Higher self at the top, heart center in the middle, physical plane on the ground.

I went to this aligning coach to learn how to tap into my heart center and align with my higher self. She gave me tools. But most of us are living out our lives on the physical plane. It is often a place of stress, anxiety, fear, and the ego. We are not connected to the higher self. We don't have the tools.

My aligning coach is an intuitive healer, so she has access to insights about the nature of the self. She is much like Sarah the shaman in this way. After she watched Jack move about the room for about an hour, she told me that Jack was totally connected to his higher self. He was living his life in his integrity, not grounded in the physical plane like the rest of us. She said he is one of the most joyful beings she has ever met. He is untethered to the heaviness of the ego and fear.

I thought about it and completely understood what she was saying. Jack is in constant pursuit of his own happiness and joy. He lives in the present moment. He doesn't have a mean bone in his little body. He doesn't care what people think about him. He doesn't hold judgment or grudges. From a higher-self perspective, he is living the life that I aspire to.

My aligning coach went on to explain that Jack and I needed to meet in the middle. I had to move up the hierarchy, live more from my heart center, and connect to my higher self. Jack needed to come down a bit and be more grounded on the physical plane. I thought that was a perfect description of the work to be done.

Children with autism get this higher-self stuff. They live in the present. They do what makes them happy. They do not need to conform to societal norms. In many ways, they model what we evolving humans are seeking.

There is an aspect about these children that is bigger than what we can see in the physical plane. There is a brilliance about them, a truth that emerges when we look for it. They are already on their way to finding the wholeness for their soul. Perhaps we can step back and consider this wholeness of who they are and ponder what they might be trying to teach us.

Perhaps they aren't as broken as we first thought.

Why These Children Are Here

One day, I had an appointment to speak with the director of the largest annual autism conference in the United States. We were to speak so that I could pitch my story, as I hoped to be considered for a speaking spot. I wanted to share my beliefs about children with autism. The director of the conference was a mother to two children with autism, so my impression was that she would welcome the conversation.

I gave her my background and credentials, and quickly went into my message.

"I would like to change the autism paradigm from perceiving it as a terrible tragedy to embracing it as the gift that it is," I said.

"It *is* a horrible tragedy and what you are saying would negatively impact the lives of many families!" she seethed. "We have fought hard against the pharmaceutical companies and the government to get more resources for families struggling with this illness. What you are saying would deter from the momentum we have going. Autism is *not* a gift."

I could almost feel her hands around my throat as she made her point.

With that I told her I was in no way intending to take away from all the good work they had done. I reframed what I was saying so she could understand it in a way that made sense to her. I succeeded to some degree. When we hung up, her guns were down, but needless to say I won't be speaking at her conference any time soon.

That conversation stopped me in my tracks. The viewpoint of this mother is undoubtedly justified based on her experience, which I would never argue against. I have not walked in her shoes. However, something struck me when I hung up the phone. What must it be like to live in a household with such strong beliefs about the tragedy of autism? That's some heavy energy.

I know what most people think about autism. I see how people stare at Jack when he behaves in an especially aberrant way. I see their embarrassed and apologetic looks when they catch themselves staring. People view children with autism as victims of a terrible disorder.

Autism is believed to be a mental illness with no known cure. It is considered a lifelong disorder. I know how powerful these beliefs are, but those are particularly dire labels. I was one, among many, who subscribed to them early on.

But it is only one perspective and, quite frankly, it did not serve me or my son to hang on to those beliefs. But I will admit, I did not wake up one morning deciding to change my beliefs about autism (although one can). It was a process that unfolded over time and began with Sarah the shaman.

Sarah touched on Jack's presence from the perspective of his soul. This is something I never would have considered if I stayed focused on fighting the disorder from a physical perspective. But I was open to other possibilities because I wanted so desperately to understand my son and help him connect with others in a meaningful way. So over time, I sought answers.

One door opened another, which opened another, and so on. It became apparent to me as I received more insights from many different practitioners and healers that perhaps children with autism have a bigger purpose here. Perhaps they are not the victims we thought they were.

The enormous rise in autism rates has really become a cause for concern. The following is data on autism from the Centers for Disease Control (CDC), citing the rate of the number of children who have been born with autism in their respective years:

Year	Rate
1975	1 in 5,000
1985	1 in 2,500
1995	1 in 500
2001	1 in 250
2004	1 in 166
2007	1 in 150
2009	1 in 110
2012	1 in 88
2014	1 in 68

In less than 40 years, the rate has increased from 1 in 5,000 to 1 in 68. Those are quite the numbers. They are causing alarm and fear in parents and communities. But what is it that's happening?

Why is autism increasing at such epidemic proportions? There are two different ways we can respond to these questions.

One way we can consider this development is that these children are a product of an overburdened, toxic environment. It is pretty easy to correlate the level of increasing pollution in our air, food, and water to the toxic accumulation and body burden we are experiencing as a species. Our children, with autism or without, are profoundly affected by these circumstances.

But while every child may not be born with autism, the alarming rate at which autism is on the rise makes it seem like we will get to that point in the relatively near future. In these large numbers, can we take to heart the message that we need to make better decisions about how we live and interact with our environment? We all know that there is a better way to live. Perhaps these children will remind us of this and be the catalyst that goads us into *doing* something about it.

The other way we may consider all that is happening is from a spiritual perspective. When we look at a child with autism in relation to the wholeness of their soul, we get a much broader view of what is happening here. I have a son with autism who lives connected to his higher self. He is brilliant in so many ways, but this one fact astonishes me. I want to be more like him in this respect.

I practice daily meditation, among many different tools, so that I too can be connected to my higher self. It is an ongoing, daily discipline that requires a serious effort. A recent article in *Yoga Journal* stated that 20 million Americans practice yoga. There are closer to 30 million who meditate. I would say that there are many others like me, that there is a movement underway. Many people all over the world are waking up to their desire for a better life.

We have begun to seek more. Up until now, most of us have simply spent our life working in a job we don't love, scraping out just enough money to pay a mortgage, and just trying to stay afloat. But this status quo is not working for many of us anymore.

We want more. We want daily joy and exhilaration. We want to feel fulfilled and have a sense of purpose. We want to be happy. These are all aspects of our higher self.

Are these children really victims of a tragedy? I choose to think not. Rather, I find that they are steadily showing up in greater numbers to deliver a message that we sorely need to hear: that there is a better, higher place for us to be. They are here to be the model of what we all really want.

An intense, white light shone from above. It was brighter and more magnificent than anything I had ever seen. It lasted only a few seconds. When this light faded, the same intense white light emanated from my chest. It came from my heart center and it too faded after a few seconds.

After meeting with Sarah in Vermont, I was suddenly motivated to explore this other aspect of our being within myself. It was like a spiritual can of worms had been opened and I was intrigued to learn more. Until I met Sarah, I had never considered the purpose of my soul or that I had a higher self.

I found a shaman for myself in California. Rudy became a trusted friend who facilitated some serious healing in me. I did a lot of work with him, exploring all of the big questions and working through some heavy pain.

The white light that I experienced took place during one of our sessions. This was a spiritual experience I liken to the near-death experiences people have when they see a white light. I was not about to die, but I was in a place of deep pain and I was begging God to give me an answer.

The light that shone from above and then from within me was one of the most significant messages I had ever experienced, if not the freakiest. It was the link between God and me. It was the message that God lives within, that I have direct access to divinity. We all do.

If it were not for Jack and his autism diagnosis, I would never have come to experience that light, that knowing. All of the pieces started to fit together so nicely.

And that was a pretty cool thing to happen.

Part Two

ALIGNMENT

Chapter Seven

THE SPIRIT OF AUTISM

When Jack was three years old, we were a full year into an intense, 40-hour-per-week applied behavioral analysis (ABA) program at home. One day, I found myself watching the video feed that we had set up in his ABA therapy room. Pat was the one who reviewed the footage most evenings, so I was only just checking it in real time on a periodic basis. On the video monitor, I saw Jack's lead teacher Mark working with him as usual.

Mark was teaching Jack an aspect of the language program.

"Jack," Mark said. "Say *mmm*. Say *mmm*."

"Mm," Jack said.

"Excellent, Jack. That was awesome!" Mark then gave Jack a cookie.

"Now, Jack, say *man*. Mmman."

"Mm," Jack said.

"All right," Mark said. "We can try again. Say *man*. Say *man*."

"Mm."

"No, Jack, say *man*. Man."

Jack didn't say anything.

"Jack?" Mark said. "Say *man*."

Jack, rather than say anything, started to get out of his little seat to reach for a toy that was near Mark. But Mark held it out of Jack's reach.

"No, Jack, you can play with the toy once you say *man*. Say *man*."

But Jack reached for the toy again. And rather than keep it out of his way, Mark grabbed Jack at the top of his shoulder and forced him down into the seat.

I ran down the hall and barged into the room.

"Mark! What are you doing?" I interrupted.

"Andie, I'm really sorry. I'm really sorry. I just got really frustrated," he offered.

"Mark, you can't put your hands on my boy like that! What were you thinking?"

"I know, I know. I'm really sorry. I just feel so much pressure to get Jack to perform and there are some days that nothing goes right." He clearly felt bad.

When Jack was officially diagnosed at 20 months old, Suffolk County set up an ABA therapy program of 40 hours per week in our home. They provided certified ABA therapists who were paid through various agencies, and they would work in two- to four-hour blocks. I was of course appreciative of how much support the county provided to us—it was such an investment in resources! But I never felt quite right about the program. It was all that was presented to me and the county felt very strongly that it was the only proven intervention for children with autism. Even though there was a gnawing feeling in my gut that it wasn't the right program for Jack, I didn't know of anything else we could do.

Immediately after the incident with the forceful handling of Jack, I had Mark go home. I was really upset by the interaction. Even now it still makes me queasy when I think about it.

But the most interesting thing is how Jack reacted.

He did not seem to be bothered at all.

Applied Behavior Analysis: The Cost of Conformity

Ivar Lovaas was a clinical psychologist at UCLA. His original studies in the 1950s showed the efficacy of using aversive stimulations such as electric shock. He used these techniques to successfully treat about 50 percent of individuals engaging in extreme self-injurious behavior, most of whom were diagnosed with schizophrenia or autism. But in 1973, he published a long-term follow-up for the behavior modification intervention and was dismayed to find that most of the subjects had reverted to their pre-intervention behaviors.

He then developed different methods using nonaversive approaches for children with autism and sought to begin intervention earlier, at preschool age, and with the strong support of the child's family in the home. With this approach, he was met with greater success. His research showed that close to half of the children who underwent this type of therapy attained a normal IQ and tested within the normal range on adaptive and social skills.

Through this process he developed the Lovaas technique. The United States Surgeon General looked at 30 years of Lovaas's research and endorsed the efficacy of his technique at "reducing inappropriate behavior and in increasing communication, learning, and appropriate social behavior." Today, Lovaas is considered to be one of the fathers of what we now know as ABA.

ABA, formerly known as "behavior modification," postulates that learning is hindered by abnormal behaviors. Through positive reinforcement methodologies, targeted behaviors will increase or decrease over time. ABA is used to help individuals acquire language skills, self-help skills, and play skills. It also uses behavioral principles to decrease maladaptive behaviors such as aggression, self-stimulatory behaviors, and self-injurious behaviors.

The main technique used by an ABA therapist is called a discrete trial. This is the process of breaking down a skill and building it up, rather than trying to teach an entire skill in one go. Mark and the other therapists used ABA techniques like discrete trials with Jack on a daily basis. They taught him how to recognize colors, shapes, numbers, letters, and eventually how to read and do math. They taught him how to speak again, like the exercise from the story with the forceful handling was intended to do. If Jack was learning colors, a discrete trial looked like this:

Discrete Trial One

Mark places a yellow and a blue card on the table in front of Jack.

Mark says, "Point to yellow."

Jack points to yellow.

Mark says, "Great job, Jack!" and pauses before moving on to trial two.

Discrete Trial Two

Mark places a yellow and a blue card on the table in front of Jack.

Mark says, "Point to blue."

Jack points to blue.

Mark says, "That's terrific, Jack!" and pauses before moving on to the next trial.

In the discrete trials, if Jack behaved correctly, he would be given a reward. The line of thinking here was that if the behavior was followed by some sort of positive reinforcement, it was more likely to be repeated. For children with autism, this is usually a reward in the form of a preferred toy or food. This is how the therapists taught Jack colors, shapes, numbers, letters, categories, prepositions, and many other common items that could be identified, like a chair or a table.

And this process would go on. All day. Every day. They did the same thing with every skill they were trying to teach him. He mastered colors, shapes, letters, numbers, math, reading fluency, and spelling. He was able to learn all of these things and he also learned how to speak with ABA. We were very grateful for the progress he made over the six years we utilized an ABA program.

But Jack's ABA therapists wanted him to look more "normal."

Whenever Jack would get really excited about something, he would shoot his hands right up in the air. Picture a person startled by a police officer who yells, "Stop! Put your hands up!" That's what Jack used to do when he got excited.

So the therapists trained him to clasp his hands and hold them down between his knees. They worked on that for about a year. And it worked. To this day, Jack still complies with an ABA-taught "more socially acceptable" mannerism.

ABA has been endorsed by a number of state and federal agencies, including the United States Surgeon General and the New York State Department of Health. With the rise in autism rates over the past decade, there has been a dramatic increase in the use of ABA worldwide. It is understandable that ABA has gotten results for many children, given the intensity of working one-on-one for such extended periods of time. There is no doubt that it is effective for many children.

Pat was always in charge of the ABA program in our home. He held team meetings with the therapists, met with the school district, evaluated the data, and formulated the goals for the program. But I could never throw myself into the program with any enthusiasm. While the incident with Mark was troublesome, there was something below the surface that bothered me. I never felt it was natural to teach a child social skills using positive reinforcement. It was too rote and impersonal. But there was a lot of pressure for the ABA therapists to do these things with Jack. They had to collect data on how many times he did things right or wrong. They were evaluated on their techniques, their data, and Jack's successes.

As we've already explored in earlier chapters, one of the most significant issues children with autism face is how they don't behave as most people do. There is therefore a large drive to teach certain things, like getting them to look at other people, read body language, have empathy, and have an ongoing conversation with a friend. The ABA therapists tried to do these things, but as the incident with Mark illustrated, they are very difficult behaviors to teach in this way.

I recently read a post on the blog Unstrange Mind written by an adult with autism who underwent a decade of ABA as a child. She made a very bold statement that, based on her experience, ABA is abuse. She did not say so out of a vengeful, mean-spirited place. She felt that to function within the forceful nature of that environment, she had to squelch her own spirit. She has suffered severe emotional trauma because of the nature of her therapy. Her post was done out of her own desire to bring light to the very damaging effects this type of experience can have on a person.

When we do something because we are forced to conform to that which is purported as normal, we experience a dampening of the spirit. Or worse, a deadening of the spirit.

But ABA has some great success stories. Yes, it works with some children, maybe because of the sheer intensity of the one-on-one interaction. Or perhaps it is the blessing of having a really caring, compassionate ABA therapist. There are as many ways to do ABA as there are therapists. And as the woman above described, it can also result in the total defeat of the spirit, the giving up to compliance because the alternative is even worse.

Parents who participate in these ABA programs, as I did, have the most benevolent intentions. But are these children who undergo intense ABA enjoying the process? Do we ignore the signs that they are unhappy because we are doing something "for their own good"? Are we really more driven by making them conform to societal standards than we are interested in understanding the totality of who they really are?

Wants and Needs

Why might we create an environment for a child with autism that runs such a big risk of dampening their spirit? Why might it have been so important to Jack's ABA therapists for him to try to look normal? And what is it about the discrete trials that leads to such a rote, impersonal experience for the child and the therapist alike?

To explore this, it will be helpful to look at the act of pursuing something from a different perspective—that of playing the piano. My son Sammy is eight years old and is becoming known around town as "the eight year old that brings tears to my eyes when he plays." You see, as of this writing Sammy has been playing the piano for four years and for the last six months of that time my house has been under construction. The construction crew has heard him play every morning before school.

Sammy loves to play. He seeks out sheet music for fun songs like the song from the Charlie Brown cartoons and "He's a Pirate" from *Pirates of the Caribbean*. But he also plays Pachelbel's "Canon in D Major" and Beethoven's "Moonlight Sonata," which apparently make the construction crew a little weepy. Sammy gets into it. He feels the music and plays by ear.

In the process of being a parent to Sammy, I have traded stories with so many former piano players. More often than not, the person with whom I speak gave up playing the piano in their youth. They hated the constant pressure to practice. They regret not continuing the process, but they quit as soon as they were old enough to stand up for themselves. My husband was one of those kids. He hated it so much that the minute he was old enough, he told his parents that he was done.

We have tried hard not to become those types of parents to Sammy. Sure, we remind him to practice, but we also make it fun and we encourage him to explore new songs that he likes. And we have the most amazing piano teacher, a young man in his 20s who challenges Sammy while also making the process an opportunity to have fun. Sammy practices because he enjoys the experience of playing and he loves blowing his piano teacher's mind with his talent.

This winds up to be the essential ingredient in Sammy's pursuit: rather than be raised in a world where he is forced to play the piano, he is being raised in a world where he enjoys it. This is because we learn to hate the things we are forced to do. The more we think we *should* do something, the less we *want* to do it. Think about going on a diet or exercising more. How many people do you know who begin a diet with gleeful exhilaration? Or if someone's doctor tells him he should exercise more, do you think that person is skipping out of the doctor's office eagerly anticipating a new gym membership? Nope. He is begrudgingly doing what he thinks he *should* do, or worse, feeling guiltier and guiltier for not doing it at all. Either way, there is no joy in the "shoulds."

Perhaps the biggest, most pervasive form of discontent in the American population can be seen in the workplace. Gallup's 2013 State of the American Workplace survey cited that 70 percent of Americans hate their jobs or are disengaged from them. The number one reason they cited for this malaise was "the boss from hell."

Why are bosses so powerful? Because they have the power to decide whether or not the employees keep their job. If the employees have to keep their job in order to survive, then the boss has the ability to use force or threats in order to ensure that they keep it. There may not be actual direct force or threats in the workplace (though there certainly can be), but the mere possibility of losing a job is a powerful enough threat that people show up every day.

They show up to work because they need to, not because they want to.

Seventy percent of Americans hate their jobs or are disengaged from them! At the very least, these people feel a sense of separation from their jobs, a level of apathy. I know more about autism than I do productivity, but I am pretty sure that people who are apathetic to their jobs are not as productive as they could be. What sorts of opportunities are missed? How many people are living lives that are adequate at best? This is a heavy price to pay both to the economy and the human spirit.

On the flip side, what would the world be like if 70 percent (or more) of Americans loved their jobs? Can you think about a time that you were really inspired to do something? Did it feel even one bit like work or effort? My guess is that it did not.

I relate this dilemma to my own experience in writing this book. I do not need to write it or feel that I should write it. I *want* to write it. And as a result, I am more productive and joyful in this writing process than I've been in many other areas of my life, especially those in which I felt I needed to participate.

My spirit is lifted when I write. I feel lighter, more positive, and more joyful. This trickles over into my children's experience. My family is lighter, more positive, and more joyful because I am. One of my favorite quotes by Confucius illustrates this trickle effect:

> When the heart is set right, then the personal life is cultivated; when the personal life is cultivated, then the family life is regulated; when the family life is regulated, then the national life is orderly; and when the national life is orderly, then there is peace in this world.

As soon as Pat was old enough to quit the piano, he did. This situation plays out again and again when a child feels forced to do something rather than wants to do it. Putting pressure on a child with autism to *look more normal* may get enough traction so that a therapist can report on their form that progress has been made, but what will actually have happened to the child 10, 20, or 30 years down the road?

Just like a child quits the piano, are these children going to give up on connecting with others as well?

Why Do We Deny the Child What He Wants?

Looking at Jack fills me with wonder. I wonder what is going on in his beautiful mind. While I don't fully understand everything he does, I know he has good reason for his actions. I also know that he is living from a place of connection. He is more connected to his higher self and he is freer than almost anyone I know. When a child with autism is inspired to do things because he wants to rather than be forced to do what he needs to, we begin to see these little truths. So why do people resist the possibility of those truths being revealed?

I have never met a renowned spiritual leader like a prominent yogi or His Holiness the Dalai Lama, but I've read about the experience that people have when they meet such peaceful people. They are humbled and inspired merely by their joyful presence.

Thich Nhat Hanh, a zen master and buddhist monk, teaches that we can learn to live happily in the present moment. He states that this is the only way to truly develop peace, both within oneself and in the world. I often think about that statement and the expression of living happily in the moment, for I witness such a behavior in Jack every day.

When children with autism find ways to cope—by spinning, twirling, hand flapping, jumping, or other aberrant behaviors—we immediately get uncomfortable. We experience a strong desire to stop the behavior and teach the child to conform. But if you were to actually stop and watch a child with autism jumping up and down, flapping his hands, and maybe even squealing, and you eliminate the need to declare that it is the right or wrong thing to do, you would probably see a child experiencing joy.

The spiritual leaders advocate for simplicity. Live in the present. Find happiness in the now. And we lap it up, eager for more. So how come when our children find happiness in the now, we feel discomfort and seek to change their behaviors?

I believe it all begins with misunderstanding. People see a child's aberrant behavior as a reflection of their turmoil. And this might be true, but it also might not be true. There are some behaviors that suggest an imbalance or trouble, like covering ears or rocking back and forth. These might suggest sensitivity to sound, or maybe they've shut down because they are overwhelmed or feel anxious.

But even if a child is doing something that is joyful, like spinning an object or jumping up and down, we get uncomfortable. There is confusion and lack of understanding, and perhaps even fear. I have had conversations with people about how Jack spins things. They believe that if I don't stop his behavior, he will get stuck where he is today for the rest of his life.

We certainly have reasons for acting the way we do, just as much as our children with autism do. Remember how the boy in the high school gym ran out of the rally and how the crowd cheered when he was brought back? They were not being malevolent. They believed that in making the boy conform they were somehow doing the right thing for him.

Social psychologists are greatly interested in how we conform to societal norms. The reason they cite for why we do it can be summed up as us having a need to feel connected and understand our place in our community. But we often do this to a fault.

Bertrand Russell, the British philosopher, said that "Collective fear stimulates herd instinct, and tends to produce ferocity toward those who are not regarded as members of the herd." Perhaps this is why we want to fit in with others and are afraid to be alone—because of the possibility that if we are, we will be on the receiving end of this ferocity that Russell spoke of. Perhaps the solitary nature of a child with autism sparks some deep fears in us, creating a desire for us to avoid this outcome at all costs. Perhaps this fear is driving our fierce desire to make our children look more normal.

It is understandable that we want the best for our children. But maybe we are missing our chance to connect with these remarkable beings, and in fact are actually undermining their ability to connect with us.

A New Way to Respond

You may remember the incident I described in the introduction of when Pat got upset with Jack for waking him up and making noise in the bathroom. When I went into the bathroom to console Jack, he didn't need any consoling. He didn't internalize the anger like a typical child might. He had in fact internalized the episode, but the first thing he said had to do with promoting Pat's well-being.

He bypassed the typical response we might have (like defensiveness or anger) and jumped right into thoughts like *how can I make him feel better?*

There is so much talk around the *tragedy* of autism. The autism conference director to whom I spoke completely shocked me by her reaction to my message and her attachment to the tragedy story. But that is the going story. That's what people believe about autism.

Jack's behavior in the bathroom tells a different story. The way he reacted to his father is as aberrant in our culture as so many other behaviors of a child with autism, but what's different is that many of us aspire to that particular departure from the norm. Jack's behavior that day suggests a connection to the higher self, which is what so many of us are seeking for ourselves. The fact that there are tens of millions of Americans practicing yoga and meditation attests to this.

What if we considered this type of behavior as inspiration for a different way of living? What if we recognize that our purpose is not to force children with autism to conform to our world but to align with our own higher selves? In doing this, we would be creating a world that is closer to the ideal of unconditional love.

Unconditional love is exactly what it sounds like—*love without conditions.* But unconditional love is a funny thing. We like to say love is unconditional, but our behaviors suggest otherwise. We reserve the word "love" only for our closest friends and family, and even then we decide that we love them only if they fulfill certain expectations—like treating us a certain way and getting a certain outcome out of having them in our life. There are always expectations attached. The attachment to outcome, the expectation, is the undoing of unconditional love. The expectation becomes the condition.

We all love our children unconditionally when they are born, simply because they are our children. But we tend to start packing on the conditions as our children grow up. We require them to clean their room, do their chores, and to behave a certain way, and these are all necessary behaviors to function within a family and a community. But when the expectation that they do these things is not met, we hold ourselves apart from them. We get angry and frustrated. We withhold our love.

When someone other than our children demonstrates seemingly aggressive or contrary actions toward us, we not only withhold our love but we often feel contrary toward them in turn. We feel anger toward them, and even hatred. But if we could understand that all humans have fears, and that they're simply acting according to their underlying beliefs as based on those fears, perhaps we could approach them differently. If we could embrace that their actions are a reflection of their own suffering and turmoil, then we have the potential to love them regardless of those actions. From this place of compassion, we could truly help them.

That's a pretty tall order. But Jack demonstrated this process in action when he responded to his father's anger as an expression of pain. He knew that what his dad needed was a kiss to feel better. My son has opened me up to the possibility that unconditional love is possible, and in fact has convinced me that part of his purpose for being here is to teach me about how to create this feeling in myself. It is a message that he and many children with autism are here to share.

What if we approached our child with autism from this perspective? What if we approached *life* from this perspective?

But how would we do this? We could meet the child in his own world on his terms. We could stop trying to force him to conform to ours. We could love him unconditionally by dropping all attachment to outcome. We could establish a trusting, benevolent connection without expectation. We could learn to connect to our own higher selves so as to foster a more harmonious place to share that connection.

The next part of this book will provide you with the tools necessary to achieve this reality for yourself and your child.

I remember preparing dinner on the evening of the day that Mark got overly aggressive with Jack. I was finally focusing on something other than the incident, and I realized I had calmed down. I had been perseverating all afternoon. It felt good to have drifted away from those thoughts.

Jack was in the living room and I watched him from the kitchen. He seemed perfectly content to be playing with his toys. He was doing his usual thing of spinning the plastic parts of the toys, not interested in playing with them in the way they were intended.

On any other day during this early stage of his life, I would have felt uneasy. His aberrant behaviors were still a source of discomfort for me then. But this evening, I felt different. I was so relieved that he appeared okay. What started out as my gnawing frustration about the events of the day led to the realization that those events seemed irrelevant to him.

When I think about Jack's behavior toward Mark that day, I realize he was not only *okay* later in the day, but that he was never *not okay* after it happened. His relationship with Mark never skipped a beat. He continued to be excited to see Mark on subsequent days, and he never appeared to be fazed in the least by what happened.

Jack is not typical. This is certain. But this quality, this uniqueness, is for totally different reasons than what most people think.

Chapter Eight

JOINING OUR CHILDREN IN THEIR WORLD

April filled in as a substitute one-to-one aide for three months of Jack's year in kindergarten when his regular aide went out on maternity leave. She was assigned to work with Jack for the entire day, mostly supporting him in academic work and encouraging interaction with his peers. It was kindergarten, so there was a lot of playtime.

April recently interviewed for a position in our home program and she told me about her experiences with Jack when he was five years old. Generally, April was supposed to encourage Jack to act as normal as possible. She was supposed to stop aberrant behaviors in favor of normal behaviors. She knew this was what was expected of her, but there was one particular day when they were on the playground in which she felt moved to abandon protocol and go with her gut feelings. For some reason she just felt like having a really good time with Jack and following his lead.

Jack loved to swing in circles on the tire swing. And he also loved to just spin the tire swing and watch it go round and round. Normally, she would stop this behavior. But on this day, she decided to get really, really excited alongside of him and helped him make it spin. She squealed and jumped around with him and totally got into the moment. She said she felt so good and free, and loved interacting with him in this way.

Then they went over to the regular swings because Jack loved to swing super high. She noticed the gym teacher had been staring at her and he shot her a disapproving glance. It made her uncomfortable for a moment, but then the exhilaration she felt took over again. She decided to get really excited again, this time about swinging Jack super high. She stood in front of him instead of behind him, pushed his feet to get the momentum going, and looked into his eyes the whole time. She said they had such a great time being silly and laughing while he swung his little heart out.

As they walked into the building at the end of recess, she noticed more disapproving glances. This time, it was from a few of the other teachers. But despite that, she sensed that Jack was in a really good emotional place for the rest of the day. Usually, Jack would insulate himself from his classmates and stay in his own world. On this day, however, Jack seemed to exhibit an astonishing desire to connect with his peers. While he didn't really know how to engage with them, he followed them around and sought to sit near them and laugh. It was like the joy that he and April had experienced together triggered something in him. It opened a door to social interaction unlike anything she had seen before.

But then April described the observations she made about Jack over the next three years when she was called in to substitute. When Jack was in kindergarten, she felt a nagging uneasiness about how the joy that Jack had expressed seemed to be at the expense of abandoning the regular protocol. Her instinct told her to embrace his joy, but what would happen if people in her position only stopped the aberrant behaviors? Over those three years, she noticed that Jack learned to speak better and he progressed in academics. He did math at above grade level and he read and wrote fluently. But what seemed particularly significant was that she actually saw Jack slipping away socially as the school years progressed. She commented that Jack's ability to connect with his peers diminished dramatically.

She opened a hole in my heart that day, as I momentarily considered what might have been. I had "if I only knew then what I know now" kind of thoughts. I felt sad about my earlier decisions to go with the status quo, or what the experts said was the only way to respond to a child with autism.

But then I remembered that my own gut instincts had prevailed. On this particular day I spoke to April, Jack was already one year into a new program that we ran from home because I had pulled Jack out of school at the end of third grade. I had asked myself what Jack really needed but wasn't getting, and I had concluded that the social piece was missing. I had realized that a drastic change was required.

So on that day, I shifted thoughts about what might have been for Jack to the beautiful promise of what will be in his future.

Misunderstanding Their Solitude

You may remember my explanation in Chapter 5 of how the behaviors of a child with autism are indicators of what he is experiencing in any given moment. If a child toe walks, he is likely seeking sensory input because his sense of balance is off. If a child jumps up and down while flapping his hands, he may be seeking input about where his body is in space, or reassurance that his arms and legs are actually attached to his body.

Behaviors are strong clues about a child's experience. And if we choose to be open-minded and set our fears aside, they are extremely useful for those of us surrounding the child. We have an opportunity here to help the child correct any physiological imbalances and move him toward his healthiest, most balanced state.

But what if there was something else that we could do for our children beyond facilitating their return to physical wellness? What if we could somehow interact with our children in a way that inspired them to want to share meaningful connections with others?

Many of us share the belief that autism is a disease that cripples the child's brain and body and compromises his interest and ability to connect with others. We look at it as a behavioral disorder that must be managed by stopping behaviors. And we don't hold much hope for these children to develop any meaningful relationships.

I remember my mentor Sid Baker explaining his thoughts about expectation to a mother who could not see her eight-year-old son as ever being toilet trained. She lamented over the difficulty of raising a child with autism and how it was compounded by the fact that he still wore diapers.

"If you hold the bar down low," Sid said to her, "your child will meet you there. But if you hold the bar high up here, your child will rise to the occasion."

This resonated with me. Generally, we really don't expect much of children with autism and we certainly don't believe they can have joyful, productive lives full of meaningful relationships. As a result, our children are trapped in a world of limitations. Their futures are grossly limited and their potential is minuscule at best. Many of us never think to raise the bar up high, for we settle for what we have been told to believe.

The Reason I Jump is an immensely popular book written by 13-year-old Naoki Higashida, who is a boy with autism. At one point in the book, he poses a question: What's the worst thing about having autism? In his response, he speaks to the misery he and children like him ultimately feel. But he doesn't claim that this misery comes from his hardships in and of themselves. He states that the reason that he gets as sad as he does is because his presence causes grief for those around them. Because he causes problems for others and is capable of doing so little, he finds that he is the source of other people's pain. And that's what he finds to be so difficult—their pain causes pain in him.

Our children with autism don't look normal, so we pressure them into behaving a certain way so that they do. But as Higashida suggests, by doing this we are imposing an incredible amount of stress on our children. We are bombarding them with the message that they are causing grief to others on a constant basis. We are conveying the message that something is really wrong with them and we are experiencing grief because of it.

When we really try to get into the hearts and minds of people with autism, we will begin to see the truth of who they really are. But a heavy veil is shrouding this truth. Because we haven't endeavored to lift this veil, the obstacles in their way can seem insurmountable. Our current beliefs about them cause our experience with them to be one of sadness and pain, and the experience they have in response reflects this as well.

But what if we could choose a different belief? What would our experience be like if we found another way? What kind of life could *our children have* if we found another way? The possibility of this other way exists. It can be realized not through supplements or healing modalities but through something else entirely.

Giving the Child Permission to Be Themselves

After April changed her approach to playing with Jack, his behavior changed in turn. He had a desire to connect with his peers. When she went with her gut feeling of being playful and silly—of having fun—she facilitated his desire to be a part of the world around him. This story is a strong reflection of what is possible for children with autism.

But if April considered Jack as having a behavioral disorder, a day like that would not likely have taken place. This is why we must not consider autism to be a behavioral disorder, but rather a social relational disorder. And there is a big difference between the two.

A person with a social relational disorder struggles to connect with people and doesn't easily form meaningful relationships. At the core of this condition, the person is unable to bridge the gap between what he wants (to communicate and connect) and what he is actually able to do on his own. In other words, he needs help in learning how to connect and relate.

In contrast, when autism is approached as a behavioral disorder, it is defined as a problem that requires a shaping of behavior with heavy emphasis on stomping out aberrant ones. When we choose to change a child's behavior because we deem it bad or inappropriate, we send a very damaging message to the child. By not seeking to understand the child's reality, we miss the very thing that we want the most, to connect with our children. And furthermore, we can actually cripple the relationship in such a way that the child suffers. They experience a greater turmoil than we can even imagine.

But April did something very profound that day on the playground with Jack. She embraced a different idea. She chose not to force Jack to conform to everyone else's form of play, and instead decided to meet Jack where he was at and enter his world.

As a result, Jack opened up—even if just a little. He wanted to be around his peers. He felt compelled to follow them and be near them. It was like he got an inkling of how fun people can be and he wanted more.

April discovered something quite paradoxical that day, almost by accident. Everyone was telling her to behave in a certain way because they believed that Jack's "behavioral disorder" would get worse if he was not stopped or encouraged to change his behavior. But in fact, the opposite happened. By joining Jack in his world, April was letting him know that he was okay exactly as he was. She was acknowledging, in a sense, that his daily quest for his own personal joy (like spinning the tire swing) was not in fact a source of grief and frustration for her. And by letting herself have fun in his chosen activity, she seemed to give Jack a glimpse of how fun human interaction can be—so much so that he actually sought out more of it later in the day.

There are many ways to intervene on behalf of a child with autism. We can change the diet, add supplements, and choose healing modalities that strengthen the child's immune, digestive, and neurological systems. But there is another very powerful thing that we can do. We can intervene on our *own* behalf and change our perspective of how to interact with our child.

Sid said that when we hold the bar high, the child rises to the expectation. By changing our perspective of how to interact, we create an incredibly powerful space to help our children. We can do away with forceful tactics to change behavior and instead meet the child where he is and let that be okay.

By accepting our children exactly where they are and finding joyful ways to have fun with them, we will create a new experience for ourselves and our children that will no longer inadvertently suppress them. Instead, it will open a door to connections that we previously thought were impossible to obtain.

It will show us that people with autism have a tremendous capacity for empathy, compassion, and love.

The Son-Rise Program

Back in 1974, two parents by the name of Samahria and Barry "Bears" Kaufman had a little boy who was different. Raun, their son, would sit rocking back and forth for hours. He never made eye contact with anyone. Given the rarity of autism at the time, these two were not quite sure what they were dealing with.

Samahria and Bears visited hospitals and clinics across the country in search of ways to help their child. What they discovered was unsettling. They saw aversive actions, like attempting to control children's behaviors by tying them to their chairs or placing them in large black boxes. They sought out experts to explain what was going on with their son, but they were simply told there was not much that could be done.

After many evaluations by these experts, they were told that Raun was mentally retarded, had an IQ of 30, and would never communicate. The experts suggested that the Kaufmans focus on their two healthy daughters at home and place Raun in an institution. But Samahria and Bears decided to formulate their own method of intervention.

Samahria began by taking Raun into a distraction-free room, which in their little apartment happened to be the bathroom. She spent 12 hours per day, seven days per week in the bathroom with Raun, doing something that all the experts warned them against: she joined him in his world. Raun would rock back and forth all day, so that's what she did as well. She spent all of her time joining him in his repetitive behaviors, but she did not just copy him. She sought to understand his world and to convey the message to him that she was okay with him exactly as he was.

Day after day, Samahria joined Raun in the bathroom. She had no expectations of Raun; she just knew that she wanted to connect with her son and understand him. But day after day, they just rocked together. Raun remained insulated from his mother and everyone else.

After ten weeks of this, though, something happened. Raun did something he had never done before, not since Samahria had started this process or at any other point earlier on.

Raun looked at his mother.

It was a breakthrough that would lead to more breakthroughs, and over the course of three-and-a-half years, they would lead to Raun's flourish, intellectually and socially. It led to the formation of the Autism Treatment Center of America™, and the beginning of what is now called the Son-Rise Program®. In creating this program, the Kaufmans created a method of working with children with autism that fosters growth and social interaction from a totally accepting place. It serves as an alternative to programs like applied behavioral analysis (ABA).

When I first went to the Autism Treatment Center of America for the program's Start-Up class, I was surprised by the material presented. I had expected to delve right into the various methods and techniques taught by the program, but a large majority of the training was based on changing attitudes and beliefs. Our beliefs about autism were challenged. We were given the opportunity to view autism from a place of love rather than fear.

By embracing an attitude of love, acceptance, and nonjudgment, we welcomed the possibility of having different beliefs at all.

Once we recognized that we could choose a different belief, we got to the nuts and bolts of the program. At the core of it, we were taught to join the child in his exclusive behaviors. Then we were taught to celebrate any interaction the child gave us. And finally, we were taught how to inspire the child to participate in our world and our activities when he was ready.

The curriculum itself is a social curriculum based on four fundamentals of social development: eye contact and nonverbal communication, verbal communication, interactive attention span, and flexibility. There are five stages in the program that address these four fundamental areas. As a child masters the goals through the five stages, he becomes increasingly socially connected and learns to communicate in a deep and meaningful way.

Another cornerstone of the program is using the three E's, which stands for energy, excitement, and enthusiasm. By being super fun-loving and friendly, we create a model for enjoyable human interaction. It is by far the most powerful thing I have done for Jack.

We struggled for many years with ABA as we tried to teach appropriate social behavior. ABA utilized a positive reinforcement model for identifying colors and words, but how does one positively reinforce something far more abstract like a child's ability to show interest in another's feelings or to embrace the concept of being a friend? The Son-Rise Program has helped Jack to open these doors without us ever directly working on the things that lie behind them.

Recently, Jack and I were sitting at the kitchen counter. He was playing with a geometric shape called a dodecahedron. He loves math and polyhedrons.

He asked me, "What is your favorite color, Mommy?"

"My favorite color is yellow, Jack!" I said. I was totally excited, because it was the first time he ever asked about another person's favorite anything.

"I want to make Mommy a yellow dodecahedron," he said.

I about fell over right then and there. It was a major milestone. He had a totally spontaneous and sincere interest in what I liked so he could share something with me.

But later in the day, I was in our therapy playroom with him and he asked some more questions.

"What is Ashley's favorite color?" he asked.

"I don't know, Jack. Do you know?" Ashley is a teacher who sees him every day, and I really didn't know her favorite color.

"Ashley's favorite color is pink," Jack said. "I want to make Ashley a pink dodecahedron."

"Yes, Jack!" I said. "That would be so great!"

Then he said, "What is Janel's favorite color?"

"I don't know, Jack," I said. Janel was another teacher who worked with Jack.

He said, "Janel's favorite color is green. I want to make Janel a green dodecahedron."

This interaction was huge on so many levels. We had crossed a threshold. My son was inspired to ask questions about people he loves. He grasped the concept of being a friend and doing something nice for someone. It was beyond anything I expected and I was so excited that he was reaching out from a place from which we had previously believed he would never be able to inhabit.

The Son-Rise Program helps to foster meaningful relationships because it does not force the child to conform to a world that he does not understand but rather puts us in a place of joining them in their world first. It teaches us to connect with our children from a place of alignment with our higher selves, and to totally accept our children as they are without ever pushing against them. And by doing these things, it is powerfully effective and extremely fun to implement. Although I don't believe in there being a silver-bullet cure for autism, if people only had the opportunity to do one thing, then I would recommend that it be the Son-Rise Program. If there was a poll taken for what the single most powerful intervention for autism is, this program would get my vote hands down.

There are hundreds of children who have graduated from the Son-Rise Program, having mastered the five-stage curriculum. There are dozens and dozens of video clips that show the children both before and after they have mastered the program. Raun's sister Bryn grew up and married a man named William and the couple adopted an infant girl. Her name is Jade, and by three years old she was diagnosed with autism. Bryn and William ran a Son-Rise Program for Jade for five years. As of this writing, Jade is 18 years old, and according to her mom she is an exceptional human being experiencing all of the things a typical teenager gets to experience.

My favorite video clip is of a boy named Simon. He is 19 in the video, and he talks about his experience of having autism. His parents were told he was mentally retarded and that he would never talk. He remembers very slowly opening up as a young boy and how he felt an emerging connection to the people in his program. He describes what he felt like and the intensity of the love he felt during the Son-Rise Program years. He speaks of all of the things he hopes for in his future, including college and marriage. He talks about how the Son-Rise Program allowed him to reach out from a place that was unreachable, how this has given him the knowledge that anything is possible for him.

And Raun? He is in his 40s now. He graduated with honors from Brown University and is the kind of human being I aspire to be. He is one of the most charismatic and brilliant people I've ever seen, and he was also once diagnosed with autism. He is loved all over the world and teaches the principles of the Son-Rise Program globally. He is an inspiring reminder of the heights we can achieve as human beings when we drop our limiting beliefs.

Celebrating Their World

A few weeks after Jack's eighth birthday, I was sitting at the dining room table with him. We had gotten him a bird feeder for his birthday because we noticed he got particularly happy watching the birds in the trees. We put it right outside the living room window so we could see all the different birds up close. We all got really excited when a cardinal or blue jay came by, or Jack's favorite, the chickadee.

On this particular morning in the dining room, we could not see the bird feeder from our seat, and Jack was looking at the front lawn. He turned and looked at me while pointing outside.

"Do you see that bird on the lawn?" he said.

"Yes, Jack, *yes!*" I yelled as I jumped out of my seat. "I see the bird on the lawn! Yes, Jack, I do!"

Now, you might think my reaction was extreme. It was just a bird on the lawn! But what is important to know about that moment is that my son had *never*—not once in his eight years of life—looked at me and pointed to something that he wanted to share with me. By sharing his observation, he had acted on his desire to create a reciprocal relationship with someone else. That moment is bigger in my mind than any other milestone he had reached to that point. It was the beginning of a connection I had to my son that for many years I believed was unobtainable.

By this point, we had been running a part-time after-school Son-Rise Program for two months. And not only was this was our first breakthrough, but this kind of connection had never taken place after *six years* of intense ABA therapy. Jack was in the second grade at the time, and after another year of running the part-time program his progress was enough for me to feel confident that I wanted to go all the way with it.

When we started the program, Jack was in stage two of the five stages of the social curriculum. Ashley, one of his lead teachers, worked with him regularly and remembers how excited she got when Jack looked at her in the beginning. The moments, while they happened, were fleeting.

At the end of third grade, I pulled him out of school to run a full-time home program. Now, one year after running the full-time program, I have a completely different child. He asks and answers all kinds of questions, he makes up jokes, he laughs at our jokes, he asks about our favorite things, he recognizes when we are sad or hurt and wants to give us a kiss or hug to make us feel better, he initiates games with us, and he plays our games and activities while taking turns and following the rules. He also prefers for someone to be with him or playing with him most of the time. He doesn't like to be alone. He walks into a room, looks up at me, smiles big, and says, "Hi, Mommy!" He gets really sad when I leave the house, and really excited when I return home.

Jack has moved through the second and most of the third stage of the social curriculum. We are on the cusp of entering stage-four goals in some of the developmental areas. His progress is purely from a place inside of himself, like a natural progression of development. Nothing is ever forced and as a result he is spontaneously doing things and surprising us all along the way.

The idea behind the Son-Rise Program is driven by how we shape our beliefs and attitudes as parents and teachers. This process teaches us that we will only be successful when we shift our perspective on the child's behaviors. I can't emphasize the importance of this enough. I had to completely drop all fear and judgment of what my son was doing and learn to fully accept who he is. I had to let go of all expectation of outcome and remain firmly grounded in the present moment. It is a process that works on so many levels, for both the parent and child. It is a process that heals.

A child with autism is capable of tremendous empathy and warmth, and this is a huge contradiction to the going beliefs about these children. When we allow them to live in their joy, we can foster the connection, build the bridge, and watch them emerge from their isolation.

Sammy was born at the very time Jack was diagnosed with autism. I have wondered if the sadness we felt was somehow internalized by him, because he has always had this knowing about Jack that he was different. Sam acts like he is the big brother, not Jack. He is extremely protective and tolerant of Jack.

Ben, on the other hand, was born when Jack was five years old. He has another perspective. He gets angry that Jack can't be a *proper* big brother. In his mind, a proper big brother would shower him with attention, and perhaps this is because he is the baby. This frustration he experiences is pretty typical, as he, like many, doesn't feel he can relate to Jack. But I do know that Ben wants desperately to connect with his brother.

One day about a year ago, all three boys were swimming in our pool. I was sitting on the deck watching them. Usually, Ben would try and coax Jack into playing with him, typically giving up after several unsuccessful attempts.

But on this day, Ben decided to follow Jack's lead. Jack jumped in the deep end, Ben followed. Jack splashed at the edge of the pool, Ben did the same. Jack swam over to the jets and splashed, Ben followed. I watched for 30 minutes as Ben followed Jack around, in and out of the pool, joining Jack in every activity.

I realized he was intuitively joining Jack, making an attempt to connect in what seemed like a last resort. And it worked. Not only did he and Jack share laughter and fun, but there was an easiness, a lightness, about the interaction that I had never witnessed between the two.

And Ben had fun—a lot of fun. There was no forcefulness, no frustration. My four-year-old boy demonstrated to me the power of acceptance. For those 30 minutes, Ben joined Jack in his world and they had a really good time.

☆ ☆ ☆

Chapter Nine

FREEING OURSELVES OF PAIN

I arrived home from California on a red-eye flight into New York. When I pulled into my driveway, Sammy and Ben came running out the back door. They met me at my car door and squealed as they jumped up and down. Our dog Abby was with them too, unable to contain her excitement. This was a typical routine for us, as this is also what they did when I came home from working a 24-hour shift in the ER.

Usually when I returned from work or a trip, Jack was somewhere in the house playing alone. I would come to him to say hello. But on this day he was waiting at the door for me. He stood there smiling and watched everything I did.

I had been in California to see my shaman, Rudy. Another mother had recommended that I see him. She was holistic in her approach to healing her autistic son, but she was very focused on healing herself as well. I had wanted to somehow sort through the darker aspects of my demons, as I felt like I was suffocating. I wasn't living a full life; I was being choked by my fears and judgments instead. But I had no idea how to find someone to help me sort through my stuff. So when my friend recommended Rudy to me, I welcomed the opportunity. I was raised in California, so the trips back were a welcome return to my favorite state.

I call Rudy my shaman, although he is really a hybrid healer because he mixes hypnosis, meditation, and drumming and chanting with other methods to uncover issues that are blocking the whole self.

Rudy and I would always set an intention for our session. I would meditate prior to seeing him and ask my higher self to help me pinpoint the next layer of work that needed to be done. On that day, we set the intention to go into this pain that had been suffocating me. It felt rather nonspecific, but I knew there was this big pile of heaviness, like a dark density, that was surrounding me and causing me to feel a lot of fear.

As I felt this heaviness, I also realized that I'd been carrying it around for many years without even knowing it. Rather than defining or acknowledging it, I simply ran away. I had never sought out any guidance or tools that would help me realize that my psyche needed some help.

That is, of course, until Jack's presence showed me another way to live.

Based on the work I did before my session, this day with Rudy was going to be a session where I went into the pain with the intention of understanding it, acknowledging it, and releasing it. We started with deep breathing. I lay down on his therapy table and concentrated on my breath as he lit sage and other herbs to clear the energy. Then he played Native American music featuring flutes and drums.

He guided me toward the pain through hypnosis. I always felt safe in his presence, like I could meet my demons head-on with him supporting me. We began the dialogue.

"What do you feel?" Rudy said.

"I feel really cold and scared," I said. I was shivering.

"Don't be afraid," Rudy said, "the shivering is your body feeling the fear. Just keep breathing."

"Okay, I'll try."

"What do you see?"

"I see darkness. Black tendrils weaving all around me."

"Just observe them. Don't run from them. You are safe here."

"I am watching them. They are really cold and ugly."

We paused, so he could let me sit with the images. This would help me to no longer run from them.

"What do you think the darkness means?" Rudy asked me a moment later.

"There is no love here. There is no love."

"Why not?" Rudy said. "Why is there no love there?"

"This is Hell. Where is God? God is not here."

"Where is God?"

"I don't know. Why is God not here? Why did God leave me?"

"What do you mean?"

"When I was little, a child, I felt like there was no love. There was no God."

At this point, Rudy moved me through the process to come out of the hypnotic state. And as I came out of the hypnosis, I came out of the darkness as well. I left it behind. I remember very distinctly feeling the comfort of not being in that dark place anymore. I had this thin sheet wrapped around me and it was the most glorious feeling in the world. I felt so elated to be out of that darkness that I actually felt like the sheet was God. It wasn't a male, vengeful deity like is often portrayed in religious texts. It felt more like a divine intelligence or an all-powerful source energy.

Love. In that moment, I felt intense love.

"God is love," Rudy said. "Without love there is no God. There's just darkness. You've said your childhood was absent of love. You had a lot of darkness."

As I processed the session, I began to have clarity. The sheet was the reminder that God was everywhere. God was in the cool hardwood floors and in Rudy's cat as he purred and lay next to me. I realized that God is never absent.

After my session, I felt tremendous relief as the weight was lifted. It was like nothing I had ever felt before in my life. I felt safe, as if all of the pain I had felt from believing I was not loved was just an illusion. Through this shift, I changed a false belief about my very existence.

As I drove the hour home from the airport, I was struck by the fact that I was tired but exceptionally peaceful. This was an enjoyable contrast to the anxiety I had felt during my departure as I anticipated the work of addressing something buried in my subconscious.

I may have typically found Jack playing alone when I returned from a trip. But when I arrived home on this day, he stood at the door smiling.

Peaceful. That was how I described his smile in that moment. This peaceful smile with which he greeted me suggested an ease about him. He seemed like he felt safe just like I did, like some of his anxiety had dissipated with mine.

It was clear that he had experienced the shift as well.

The Problem of Limiting Beliefs

My work with Rudy in California has always put me in a better place emotionally. I have discovered that examining my life in this way—uncovering my buried fears—has allowed me to heal and align with my higher self. Despite the things that have come up, like not feeling worthy, feeling unlovable, believing I'm a burden, and even fearing that it was *not* okay that I exist, once I acknowledged them I experienced some powerful healing. I have always left California feeling lighter, more optimistic, and clearer on my life.

We all have stories from our past, and no matter what the hardship or trauma, we hold on to the pain from these experiences. And when we hold on to this pain, we develop a false sense of who we are and what we are capable of. This is the cycle of the perpetual state of fear within which many of us live. But it is an illusion.

Have you ever known someone who tries too hard in a relationship, perhaps in the early stages? That person falls head over heels, is totally available, and is ready to do anything to make her new mate happy. But then the relationship ends, probably because the person has come across as really needy. What might be driving these people? They believe that they must make themselves available in this way because they are unworthy otherwise. They have a fear of loss, abandonment, or, yes, unworthiness.

Or how about the bully on the school playground? I remember a boy in elementary school who bullied and scared a lot of kids. He was tough, and he didn't care who he hurt. We eventually discovered that his parents were divorcing and—it's obvious in retrospect—he was in pain. He had no power at home and believed that he had to bully others to reclaim that power. His behaviors were a manifestation of his pain.

If we hold on to our pain, no matter how big or small, we will sabotage ourselves. When we remain in this holding pattern, we ensure ourselves our continued suffering and turmoil in the form of fear, anger, sadness, grief, and other burdensome feelings. We continue to believe in our being a burden, in our lack of worthiness, that our only way to be powerful is to harm others.

This does not make for a very joyful life.

On the surface, my childhood was a perfectly good one. I had two parents. My father worked as an engineer and my mother stayed at home. For much of my life, I never gave any thought to the idea that my childhood was traumatic. But from an early age, I did some troublesome things.

I was 13 the first time I got drunk. I hung out with a bad crowd. My best friend liked to shoplift and we often drank at parties. We frequently cut classes at school and engaged in reckless behavior. We would sneak out of our parents' houses at night to go to parties and drink. The first time I tried drugs, I was only 15 years old.

It got worse as I got older. When I was 17, I dated a boy who was physically and emotionally abusive. He was frequently violent and even broke my hand during one fight, but I stayed with him for three years all the same. And we did a lot of drugs together. I barely remember that time of my life.

In my 20s, I had one bad relationship after another. I thought very little about what I was doing. But when I was 27, I met Greg. He was the first real love of my life. We spent a year together mostly hiking, mountain biking, running, and Rollerblading. We went on trips together, cooked together, and simply loved being with each other. It was the first normal relationship of my life.

I was 28 when the relationship ended. I could not contain the overwhelming grief. For two weeks, I drank day and night, and then finally tried to kill myself. I swallowed a handful of pills with a bottle of wine. But it didn't work.

Somehow, I pulled myself together. I had already decided I would pursue medical school and it was time for classes to start. I spent two years getting the premed requisites out of the way, and successfully entered medical school at age 30. My parents were really proud of me.

By the time I had Jack at age 38, I was pretty detached from who I really was. My work with Rudy pointed me back to my child-hood, which explained a lot about my behavior. When a child does drugs and drinks to the extent I had, allows her boyfriend to abuse her, and tries to commit suicide because a relationship ends, something rather disturbing is going on.

My parents fled Germany in 1951. My father fought in World War II at the age of 18, and my mother was just 17 when Dresden, her home, was firebombed. They fled to Canada, then moved to the United States about a year before I was born. By then, my mother had four other children, no friends, and a strained rela-tionship with her own mother.

I remember how she used to casually say that she never want-ed my sister and me—her fourth and fifth children—because she was too overwhelmed. She felt all alone, and she raised us without any support. When I asked her if she loved us, she replied that, of course, she eventually learned to love us.

My parents were very typical German parents, and they believed children should obey their parents at all costs. Their actions aligned with the proverb, "Children should be seen and not heard." My mom also accepted the prevailing sentiment of the time that said the best approach to a sobbing infant was to let him "cry it out." I don't remember my mother ever holding me as a child and saying she loved me. I was in my 20s the first time she said it. She was so burdened with the pain in her own life that she really didn't know how to nurture me.

My parents were great at providing everything else we needed, like shelter, food, and clothing. But they were teenagers in World War II Germany, and there wasn't a whole lot of emphasis on nurturing. They were in survival mode.

By the time I was five, I had been trained to not rock the boat or express my feelings. I had to be good, quiet, and perfect. One time my favorite toy was stolen from me at school, but I sat in my room and cried by myself, terrified of telling my mother. And so I embodied that perfection all those years, until I became a teenager. I rebelled like many children do in adolescence, though my father reached out to me on a few occasions. He was pretty worried about my behavior.

I imagine that my childhood is not that different from the childhoods of other children of immigrant families. But what is more significant than that is the fact that my specific experiences led to my holding on to serious pain—which in turn led to certain limiting beliefs about my unworthiness. Each of us has experienced pain of one kind or another, and if we don't free ourselves of this burden then we perpetuate our suffering throughout our lives.

Our Suffering and Autism

Have you ever noticed how the topic of human suffering pervades our world's religions, Western psychology, and other systems of thought? Judeo-Christian scriptures are full of passages that interpret the meaning of human suffering. They describe it to be a punishment for sin or evil, a test for fidelity, an occasion for God to show mercy and love, and a redemptive act by which Jesus took on all human suffering through his own death on the cross.

Buddhism is based on the four noble truths, which define our lives in the context of human suffering. The first truth states that life is suffering. That's a pretty strong statement on which an entire philosophy is based.

Shamanism is based on a practice that fully focuses on healing the human condition through access to the spirit world. Practitioners of this system believe that when we encounter a trauma, our soul fragments or splits off. Part of their role is to help retrieve and mend these fragmented parts of ourselves.

The word "psychology" is derived from the Greek words "psyche," which means soul, and "logos," which means study. Western psychology is the scientific study of the human mind and its functions, especially those affecting behavior. When people visit a psychologist they are usually seeking help with some level of pain and suffering.

Humans suffer. We experience life and inevitably we suffer. But more than that, our suffering usually impacts those around us. Most of us will have memories of when we were in a particularly dark space and this quality somehow brought down the mood of those around us. I have found that my pain and suffering directly correlate to the vibe in my household, and this idea is supported by various clichés we have in our culture, like "when Mom's happy, everyone's happy."

All children feel the truth of the emotions of the adults surrounding them. A parent might make an effort to hide troublesome emotions from her children, but children are little mirrors of us. They watch us, learn from us, and emulate us. They take on our feelings and they learn how to be in this world based on what we teach them. Most would agree with this. It's not hard to make the correlation between a parent's behavior, mood, and overall energy and a child's behavior, mood, and energy.

But this is even truer in a child with autism. We can pretend to be happy around children with autism, but they will catch on. In all of the stories I have read by individuals with autism, it is clear that they have a strong empathic nature despite their outward behaviors. On the surface, these children might appear disconnected from us as demonstrated by aberrant behaviors like rocking back and forth. But if we are in a state of distress, they might be rocking back and forth *because* we're in that state. Our imbalance becomes their imbalance, for they are much more keenly attuned to the emotional tone of their surroundings than we might think. I have been astonished by the words written by some of them. They say things about the nature of our grief causing unbearable grief in them. Or how our suffering because of them causes them to feel like they have no value. Children with autism understand on a very deep level what we are feeling, good and bad. And when we feel bad, they suffer in turn.

Pat always reminds me about Jack's noticeable, positive response to harmony in the house. He sees the difference in the way Jack opens up a little more, feels lighter, and is more connected. And as I've done work with Rudy and let go of pain in other ways, Jack has begun to express a desire to know what other people like. He asked me to tell him my favorite color so he could make me a polyhedron in that color. When I am freer, he is better able to engage.

All of this may not be news, but it is very important to consider when connecting with our children with autism. We are presented with a child who has a social relational disorder, whose best chance at forming meaningful relationships is through a process of interacting and learning from caring adults. We have to model what we want him to be. We have to give him a reason to connect. If we are heavy with despair, or feel buried in pain, we won't present a very enticing reason to engage with us.

Jack knows when I am lighter. He knows when I have released some heavy stuff. He is more willing to engage and more tuned in to my presence. I saw it the day I returned from my session with Rudy. I don't blame him. I much prefer to be with a positive, happy person as well. Who wouldn't?

It is obvious that we all want to be free of suffering. No one wants to suffer. So how do we achieve this lighter, more joyful environment for our child and ourselves?

Inner Work

You likely remember the story of Bears and Samahria Kaufman. After they created the Son-Rise Program, they founded the Option Institute™. This is a campus that the Kaufmans created in the Berkshires of western Massachusetts as a place to help people. This is where people can come to learn more about the Son-Rise Program and train in order to implement a program for the child in their life.

But a remarkable thing about visiting the Option Institute and working with the Kaufmans is that the work isn't based entirely on training for the program specifically. In the previous chapter, I alluded to how the early work of training at the Son-Rise Program's Autism Treatment Center of America had to do with shifting our attitude about autism. Though visits to the Option Institute are in many ways irrevocably linked to training in the Son-Rise methodology, much of the work that takes place when working with the Kaufmans has to do with changing our beliefs.

When I visited the Option Institute, I had been lamenting about my explosive reactions to any negativity around my house. If Pat was negative in any way, I would lose it and start a big fight.

I had a one-hour session with Bears Kaufman, where we engaged in what is known as a power dialogue. This is the method the Kaufmans developed to explore beliefs.

During the session, we explored my tendency to explode in response to negativity around the house. What we uncovered was that this behavior was the result of an underlying belief. I believed that Jack would not thrive in his Son-Rise Program if there was any level of negativity in the house. Or, more simply, I believed that my son would not succeed, period. So when something cropped up that reinforced that belief, it would act as a powerful trigger that led to my out-of-control reaction.

Humans suffer. We experience pain, trauma, and the like, and we tell ourselves stories about how circumstances, other people, or our sheer lack of good fortune are the reason why we feel the pain that we do. During our session, Bears walked me through the logic of the belief, which was clearly faulty, and I was given the opportunity to discard it. My new belief was that Jack could definitely thrive and succeed in the Son-Rise Program, regardless of anyone else's opinions and actions. I was running the program, the teachers who participated were well trained, and they all had the right attitude. I no longer freak out when there is negative commentary because my son's future is no longer attached to it. But it's important to note that my change in behavior didn't take place because there was less negative commentary. It changed because my reaction to it was different.

The process of doing inner work on ourselves is simply a training of the mind to focus differently. If we are driven to act in certain ways, especially if we don't like those ways, then we can explore what is driving us. By recognizing the belief, we are essentially determining the cause of our pain much like we might determine that a certain aspect of our child's broken physiology is the cause of his symptoms. And once we identify this cause, we can create a plan of action in response. In the case of our limiting beliefs, we do this by letting go of them. This frees us up to create a life of greater meaning and purpose.

As I have already mentioned, I was raised in an environment in which kids were "seen but not heard." But little children need their parents or caregivers to survive. In order to secure approval from my parents, I had to be quiet, do as I was told, never rock the boat, and basically live as invisibly as I could. Once I secured approval for these actions, I earned the care and attention that I needed to survive. Because I believed I needed to be invisible to survive, I grew to fear expressing my voice.

As an adult, this belief no longer serves me. I can take care of myself, so having a voice makes for a way better, more joyful experience. I was suffering in response to this limiting belief, so it was up to me to make a change. And by letting go of the fear that was held by clinging to that belief, all kinds of great things began to emerge. I began to embrace concepts like unconditional love and acceptance. They became the embodiment of who I strove to become.

Not many people understand the sheer power of our beliefs. Doing inner work on ourselves enables us to shift our mind into a place of greater acceptance, understanding, and peace, and when we decide to consciously change a belief, we can use it as a tool to shift our feelings and behaviors as a whole. And my session with Bears allowed me to do just that.

It is not hard, then, to make the jump to how our own relationship to limiting beliefs impacts our children and our families. Jack always feels the shift in me when I return home from my sessions with Rudy. This happens because I emanate warmth and well-being. By letting go, we perpetuate these qualities rather than fear. Which kind of home do you want?

Self-Love Leads to More Love

I have done some pretty crazy things in the pursuit of personal growth. I say "crazy" because many of the choices I have made would have seemed preposterous at earlier times in my life. For example, doing past-life regression therapy was so far out that I would have laughed, and hard, at anyone who suggested I try it. But everything I have done unfolded in a very natural way and made perfect sense when it arrived.

My first inkling toward healing myself and beginning inner work started with mainstream alternative therapies. I dove into acupuncture, homeopathy, yoga, and meditation. There was enough science behind some of these modalities that I did not have to stretch my belief system very far to invest in their effectiveness.

I also began to use herbs and supplements and adjusted my food intake to a more organic, whole-foods-based diet. It was a natural progression for me because I was so invested in these things for my children. I removed chemicals and pollutants from my household, got rid of cordless phones, and minimized electromagnetic radiation. These made sense to me because of all the research I uncovered related to autism, but they contributed to my wellness as well.

My inner work repertoire is comprehensive. I use different modalities when the mood strikes me or when a particular issue comes up that would be well suited to one or another process. I embraced neurofeedback in 2011, and I still use it regularly for myself and my entire family. I have been an energy-work enthusiast for several years now and love working with chakras, crystals, and essential oils. The nurses I work with at the emergency room have become my dear friends, and we laugh at each other during the full moon because we all like to cleanse our crystals. We call each other "goddess sisters" and, yes, we are perceived as a little kooky. Most recently, I got into the more esoteric stuff like shamanism, hypnosis, and past-life regression therapy. They have all played a role in understanding a piece of myself.

My life has changed dramatically as a result. My marriage gets better and better. We both understand the power of our beliefs and how the nature of our behavior is tied to these beliefs. One of the most amazing things that has happened to me in understanding my limiting beliefs is that my life has opened up into one far better than I could ever have imagined. My relationship with my children gets better and better. There is more harmony in the house.

Doing inner work on ourselves is a very personal decision. We all have different preferences and issues, even if there is some overlap. It is much like our approach to intervening on our child's behalf, in that we require a customized plan specific to our child's needs. Similarly, we must customize when we consider our own particular healing program. What works for me might not necessarily work for you.

So where do you start? That depends on where you are today. Start with something that doesn't seem like it would be a stretch for you to believe in its effectiveness. For example, if you have never considered concepts like reincarnation, you would not likely jump into past-life regression therapy. My suggestions begin with the more concrete and culminate with the more esoteric.

I encourage you to take a look at the wellness of your home environment. Eliminate any potential chemicals or pollutants in the air, water, furniture, carpets, and cleaning supplies. Then consider a diet that is as much organically based as you can afford, or at least GMO-free. Consider eating whole foods instead of processed ones, and have an evaluation by a medical practitioner for any nutritional deficiencies you may have. Then you can make choices about supplements, herbal medicine, and homeopathy if it makes sense to you.

Next, consider some form of energy shifting practice that promotes relaxation and stress-reduction. This might include yoga, acupuncture, neurofeedback, and any physical exercise that is enjoyable.

I believe that meditation is the single most powerful inner work tool available to us. It is free, it can be done virtually anywhere, and it taps into the most profound resource we have—our inner self. When we train ourselves to look within, we have access to the answers to every question we could possibly ask.

There are many energy healing modalities that can add to our meditative experience. Chakra balancing, essential oils, and Reiki are just a few of the many adjunctive therapies we can use.

Once you have experimented with these modalities, consider moving into the more esoteric. Hypnosis can provide some deep understanding and it is much easier than you might expect. I never believed I could undergo hypnosis, but with the right practitioner I found it to be enjoyable and easy to practice. Past-life regression therapy is interesting and can be very healing for some. It can provide insight into issues that might otherwise seem elusive. Working with a shaman can also be cathartic, especially when seeking clarity on a particular issue.

Pain, fear, and limiting beliefs do not serve anyone unless they are released. In the releasing of these negative emotions, we create something new. We create a space for something positive and uplifting. There are many healers, spiritual coaches, and resources today that can help us to do this.

When you do this inner work, you can create a whole new environment in which you and your children can thrive.

🧩

Recently, we placed a new computer in our dining room. It was a video-surveillance system that allowed us to have state-of-the-art video monitoring in our Son-Rise Program playroom. It was a key tool for giving feedback to my teachers and also for ongoing evaluation and development of Jack's program.

One morning I walked down the stairs to find Jack standing over the computer, laughing. When I saw that Jack had a large red cup in his hand, I knew immediately what had happened.

Jack loves fans because, of course, fans spin. This computer had a metal fan that was visible through the grid of the housing mechanism. When you pour water on a fan, it spins. As soon as I approached Jack with the cup in his hand, I saw that, sure enough, there was a large puddle on the table and water spilling onto the ground.

That was why Jack was laughing. He always laughs when he makes a fan spin.

He used to love to spray our air-conditioning units on the side of the house with the hose. He could get the blades of those giant fans to spin round and round. This would happen until we caught him and stopped him because it was dangerous for him to be near the air conditioner.

So on this morning he found a clever but expensive way to make the computer fan spin. In days gone by, I would have had a mini meltdown the moment that I realized what was happening. But instead, I felt an amazing sense of calm.

The $4,000 computer was ruined, and I chose not to explode. This is because my response to any situation is my point of power. It is where my control over my happiness lies. By doing my inner work, I had learned that my happiness—or lack thereof—was not tied to any external situation. It was only tied to how I responded to the situation. This computer incident was a powerful reminder of this fact.

When I sat with my feelings about what just happened, the only anxiety I felt was over how my husband would react. But everything worked out in the end. Computers break. We got a new one.

But now I have it locked safely in a cabinet.

Chapter Ten

BELIEF TRUMPS EVERYTHING

Jack loves puzzles. One afternoon, when I would be spending three hours with him, I brought a United States map puzzle into the playroom with me. There were 50 pieces, one for each state, so it was an easy puzzle to put together. He liked to guess the state capitals, and his keen memory ensured that he always got them all right.

Jack loved to spread all the pieces out, flip them right side up, and pick out his favorite states first. He loves New York and California because he knows we live in New York and that I was raised in California. So he went about sorting the pieces.

I was on the floor with him, excited to do the puzzle. But instead of putting the pieces on the map, he began picking up the pieces and dropping them one by one as he kept his ear close to the ground. I had seen him do this a countless number of times with lots of things. He loved dropping plastic things like Lego bricks, Monopoly houses and hotels, or pens that he dismantled. He would listen closely to the sounds they made as they hit the floor. It was a typical activity for Jack, and I had joined him many times in doing it.

Then he began to hold the pieces up to his ear, scratching and rubbing them. The ecstatic look on his face suggested that he was thoroughly enjoying the sounds they made. I watched as he repeated this with each state. He was fond of the rustling sounds that plastic, paper, cardboard, fabric, or any material that was within reach could make, so this was a typical Jack activity as well.

I decided to have some fun and expand on this little game he had going in order to challenge him a little. I grabbed a stack of puzzle pieces and put them behind my back.

"Jack, I have a really fun idea. Can you tell me what state this is?" I dropped the first one behind me, which made a small clunk as it hit the floor.

"Wyoming," he offered.

I turned around to see.

"Wow, Jack, it *is* Wyoming! That was great. How about this one?" And I dropped another.

"Kentucky."

Sure enough, it was Kentucky. We continued playing this game for a bit longer. Jack never missed a state. I decided to up the ante.

"Can you guess which state this is, Jack?" I held one piece behind my back and scratched it.

"Washington," he said almost instantly.

"How about this one?" I said, moving on. "Which state is this?"

"North Carolina."

He continued the game with me, always giving me the correct answer. I had found it remarkable when he was able to use his perfect pitch to discern five different notes being played on the piano by his brother Sammy all at once. But this just catapulted him, in my mind, to some other level.

What could possibly be going on in his reality? What were his perceptions truly like? And what was the significance of such an astute ability? I wondered what it all meant as I, once again, stood in awe of my little boy.

The Power (and Problem) of Beliefs

I would like you to try a little exercise. Think about something this very moment. Maybe it is about what you are reading, maybe it is what you will have for dinner, maybe your thoughts are wandering from one item to another, or something else. Then, put a label on the thought. Is it significant, trivial, passive, aggressive, positive, negative, or a different quality?

We all have thoughts, all the time. Some say we have 60,000 thoughts in a day. That's a lot of thoughts. They bombard us constantly. But have you ever stopped to notice the nature of what you are thinking about? There is usually an underlying feeling or quality about each of these thoughts, and primarily they could be considered either positive or negative. Have you noticed that, depending on what you are thinking about, you may feel especially good or bad?

For example, thinking about sipping coffee on the deck of a beachfront vacation home while the sun rises will provoke a very different feeling than thinking about how you are going to tell your best friend that you saw her husband with another woman. In the first case, you are probably smiling and feel pretty serene. But in the second case, you have a knot in your stomach and you feel a little queasy.

Along similar lines, consider a child who is raised by an alcoholic parent. The parent constantly belittles and criticizes him. What view do you think that child will have of himself? Contrast that child with one who is raised by fairly conscious parents. These parents consistently tell the child that he can do or be anything he wants, that he is a really good person with unlimited potential. This person would likely have a very different view of himself as an adult than the child born to the alcoholic.

Beliefs, to a large degree, make us who we are. They are the glue, the stuff that binds our identity to us. But perhaps more significantly, our beliefs trigger our thoughts, which trigger our actions. Consider the thoughts of the child of the alcoholic parent above. If the father tells him that he is stupid or lazy, then there's a good chance he'll start to believe what he's being told. He believes he is stupid so he never applies for a job that he really wants. He tells himself that he could never get the job, he's not smart enough, and he would probably fail anyway. His feelings surrounding these thoughts are heavy. He is sad and hopeless.

Now consider the other child. If he believes what his parents told him, then he will have a positive view of himself. He sees a job opening and he begins to see himself winning the job. He tells himself he would be a great candidate because he knows he can do anything he sets his mind to. He feels confident and hopeful. His thoughts lead him down a path of success and the feelings that follow this thought process are in stark contrast to the child of the alcoholic.

We as human beings suffer because of what we believe. We believe we are not good enough to get a better job. We believe we are not worthy of a mutually respectful relationship. We believe we have to adhere to the status quo. We believe in authorities outside of ourselves, like what doctors tell us or what the experts have to say. We have a lot of limiting beliefs that are based in fear and we are both individually and collectively limiting our potential.

These beliefs have the impact that they do because they form the basis of the quality of thoughts we have in any given moment. The thoughts then lead to feelings, such as uplifting, life-affirming feelings or hurtful, destructive feelings.

But just because the child of the alcoholic was told by his father that he was stupid, and he believed it growing up, is he required to continue believing such things as an adult? Or is he free as an adult to decide he is *not* stupid? The essential, even cool thing about beliefs is that we get to choose those beliefs—and therefore we get to choose our thoughts.

Think about the beliefs surrounding the diagnosis of autism. Autism is believed to be a tragedy. That is a devastating, limiting belief for the child and the family to experience. At my first Son-Rise Program training, Bears told us about a man who was the father of a girl with autism. He believed it was a tragedy. He then took a gun and shot his daughter in the back of the head as she slept. Then he turned the gun on himself and killed himself. A recent cover story of *New York* magazine was all about a mother who attempted to kill herself and her teenage daughter with autism. She did not succeed, which is fortunate, but the tragic ripple in her family will be felt for generations.

After Bears told us that horrifying story, he posed a question to the parents or caregivers of children with autism in the room: What would our belief about autism be if the following scene took place:

"Hello, I am here with my son. I need your help."

"Okay, great. Why do you need my help?"

"My son has autism."

"Congratulations! Do you know how blessed you are?"

It was a bit of a spoof, but Bears was still serious. I think about Jack and all the other amazing stories I have heard and read about. They have remarkable capabilities that are far from tragic, like how my son can distinguish cardboard puzzle pieces by sound. This ability of his can seem like a pretty cool trick that, if nothing else, could be an opportunity to dazzle others.

But really, he has provided a doorway to a whole other aspect of our reality.

Seeking a Higher Frequency

Einstein said that "everything in life is vibration." This is because everything we see around us is vibrating at one frequency or another. In this way, sound is a form of energy, just like electricity and light.

And everything else is energy as well.

We have the opportunity to explore how everything in our universe is energy through the study of quantum physics. This discipline (also known as quantum theory or quantum mechanics) is the study of the behavior of matter and energy at the molecular, atomic, nuclear, and even smaller microscopic levels. Max Planck, Albert Einstein, and Niels Bohr were among the first scientists to develop this field of physics.

Quantum theory teaches us that fundamental particles exist only in an undefined state of potentialities. They come into existence once a mind interacts with them and gives them meaning. In other words, it is necessary for a mind (with a thought, an intention) to create physical reality.

And just like sound is vibration, with different sounds having different frequencies, so too are thoughts. Thoughts are vibration, and different thoughts have different frequencies. I became intrigued by quantum physics when I was searching for some science behind the laws of the universe as it relates to energy, frequency and vibration, and, more specifically, thoughts. When we correlate the vibrations of different thoughts, we enter the science behind our beliefs.

David R. Hawkins, M.D., Ph.D., is the man who bridged the gap between science and spirituality. A renowned psychiatrist, physician, and researcher, Dr. Hawkins is uniquely qualified to present spirituality that is scientifically compelling. He created the Map of Consciousness as a tool to overcome limitations of the human mind and undue human pain and suffering. It assigns a frequency to human emotions, which are called "attractor fields." Attractor fields are nonphysical energy fields generated by an individual's attitudes, beliefs, and ongoing thought streams.

The Map of Consciousness is a scale that assigns frequencies to a whole range of emotions. This scale begins with lower-frequency emotions like blame, despair, hate, and scorn, and the lowest-frequency emotion is shame at 20. The scale continues up to higher-frequency emotions like trust, forgiveness, understanding, reverence, and bliss, with love coming in at 500 and enlightenment topping it off at 1,000. All of the higher-frequency emotions, however, correspond to a level of higher consciousness. As we as humans evolve spiritually, we move up the scale.

With each progressive rise in the level of consciousness, the frequency or vibration of energy increases. Dr. Hawkins has attested to how the presence of emotions like love and truth has a positive effect on human muscle as well as other aspects of our physical reality. Higher consciousness radiates a beneficial and healing effect on the world. By freeing ourselves of our limiting beliefs, we are able to engage from the level of higher attractor fields (emotions). When we do this, we live in synchronicity and joy, our work is effortless and rewarding, and we experience love, peace, and abundance.

In presenting this material, it is my hope that you understand the powerful correlation between our beliefs about our children with autism and the outcome of their lives. I also hope you understand that it affects the outcome of our lives as well. If we feel optimistic, accepting, and reverent toward our children, they and we will live in joy and peace.

By changing our beliefs, we cause a cascading effect on our children, our family, our country, and our world. When viewed through this lens, autism is not a tragedy at all.

I mentioned at the beginning of this chapter how Jack is able to name the notes that Sammy plays on the piano. Because Jack has perfect pitch, he can instantly name all five notes. It's the same ability that allows him to discern which puzzle piece is being dropped or scratched. Many children with autism have perfect pitch, and many of them can likely identify the different frequencies of cardboard puzzle pieces. But they can also interpret *our* frequency. This is why children with autism require us to come from a place of love and acceptance before they will truly connect with us.

What a gift.

Creating Positive Thoughts

People with autism are 500 times more likely than the general population to have perfect pitch. They also share savant abilities—extraordinary skills not exhibited by most people—in the areas of math, memory, art, and, of course, music. Their heightened sensory abilities are telling of their perception of the world. They are much more engaged within the subtle, energetic realm than you and I are.

When I watch Jack drop a puzzle piece onto the floor and then listen with joyful enthusiasm, I realize I am watching a child who is living purely in the moment. He is aligned with what brings him joy. Many of us want to be more like him in this respect.

But it doesn't come naturally for most of us. We often have to untrain ourselves, stop worrying, and stop striving. Worry is all about information from the past inspiring fear about the future. Striving is all about attaching to a specific outcome taking place in the future. These behaviors tend to sap the joy out of our lives.

So when we follow the lead of a child aligned with what brings him joy, we shift our focus to the present moment. This can be a tall order for those of us who have been programmed to experience a perpetual state of worry and striving. And focusing on being joyful? Well, that's not that easy for most of us, either.

How do we ultimately follow the child's lead in this way? There are about a hundred zillion books on this subject, so I will try and keep it simple by narrowing it down to one task. We must ask ourselves: "What would make me feel good?" This may seem like a loaded question, but it doesn't have to be. It is a question that can be pivotal for changing our thought stream from a low frequency to a high frequency.

Remember, our emotions are an attractor field, and they emit a frequency. Higher-frequency thoughts like love and acceptance attract more of these feelings into our lives. Lower-frequency thoughts like blame and hate attract more of those feelings into our lives. It really is that simple.

So I'm suggesting you always ask yourself the question, "What would make me feel good?" What we think about translates into how we feel in any given moment. Therefore, if you are not feeling good, choose a thought that is higher up the emotional scale. And if you cannot do that during a moment in which you get really carried away with a negative thought, just stop thinking about it and look around for something general that you can feel better about.

I am a huge fan of Abraham, a group of consciousness who dialogues with Esther Hicks. They teach on the power of positive thought through a very simple but powerful life-changing system. I highly recommend their teachings, or any method for shifting your thoughts to be predominantly positive that works for you. Just remember that the real energy behind a thought is the feeling, so just saying the words is useless. You have to feel it.

This may seem overly simple, but change can be hard. If we want to foster ambitious changes like the reshaping of our thoughts, then embracing a simple action is the ideal way to move forward, as long as it's accompanied by self-discipline. If you commit to the thought *My priority today is to feel good* every day, you will see that your thoughts can be either your friend or your foe. So you need a simple method for changing your thoughts. When you do this, your beliefs will follow. Abraham-Hicks says, "Beliefs are just thoughts you keep thinking." This is indeed pretty simple.

One way to begin shaping your thoughts is to displace a low-frequency thought with a high-frequency one. Let's suppose you are having an argument with your boss. You sit down at your desk and you are steaming hot with anger. That's a pretty negative emotion and we can assume you would feel bad in this anger. But would suddenly shifting to a rose-colored view of the situation be possible while you're in that state? Not likely.

Instead, approach the process more generally. Look around your office and see the beauty in a plant, reminisce about the vacation you just had, or appreciate the electricity streaming in via electrical outlets and how connected you are to the world because of this electricity. You will find yourself halting the negative emotion and exchanging it for a better-feeling one.

When we relate the nature of high-frequency thoughts to interacting with a child with autism, it's clear that something rather significant is at stake. What do you think will happen to a child born into a family that embraces the tragedy of autism versus the gift of autism? It is the difference between one mother feeling low-frequency emotions like despair, grief, blame, anxiety, and fear versus another mother feeling high-frequency emotions like hope, acceptance, optimism, and reverence for her child and his future. Energy begets *like* energy. Thoughts are energy. And higher frequency thoughts create a higher frequency life.

The unfolding of life lies in your thoughts and beliefs, for better or worse. But you get to choose. Always.

If you watch a child with autism who is not hindered by our own low-frequency beliefs, you will see a very free, very joyful child. You will see a child living in the present moment, aligned with his higher self.

What you choose to believe about your child is *the* single most important prognostic indicator you have.

The 100th Monkey Effect

In 1952, a group of scientists studied the life and habits of snow monkeys off mainland Japan. The researchers introduced sweet potatoes, a new food to the group, by tossing them to the monkeys in the sand. The monkeys loved the sweet potatoes, but were annoyed with the gritty sand covering them.

Eighteen-month-old Imo solved the grit problem by taking the sweet potatoes to the ocean to wash them. She then taught her mother and her peers the technique. The young monkeys taught their mothers the technique in turn. Pretty soon, a large number of snow monkeys were eating washed sweet potatoes.

And then one day in 1958, a threshold was reached. A contained number of monkeys had been performing the washing, and then, almost instantaneously, all the other monkeys adopted the new procedure. Furthermore, monkeys on other islands instantaneously adopted the new procedure as well.

This story was first written about by Lyall Watson in his book *Lifetide: A Biology of the Unconscious.* He created the term "100th Monkey Effect," which has stood to imply that once a belief or idea is held by a critical mass in a species (100 in this example), the belief will be adopted by all individuals in the species. Watson suggested that the habit jumped overseas after the critical number—arbitrarily assigned as 100—was reached. He described this critical mass as an awareness that becomes the conscious property of all.

The story is largely considered a fable, but it is an interesting model for social change and the power of a critical mass. Not many people would argue against the fact that humanity has been wallowing in low-frequency energy for far too long.

Children with autism are now populating our planet at epidemic rates. The situation has reached a critical mass. But really, so has our situation as a whole. We are polluting the planet and our bodies, we are filled with anger and fear toward cultures and people who are different from ourselves, and we are apathetic to the plight of our fellow human beings. Our daily lives are full of stress, anxiety, and fear.

We have work to do. One by one, we can shift our beliefs about ourselves and our world. Then we can reach a new critical mass, one that is positive. We must start with our thoughts. We must shift from predominantly negative, low-frequency thoughts to life-affirming, high-frequency thoughts. By practicing trust, forgiveness, acceptance, and love, we will raise the energy in our homes as well as our planet.

When we reach this positive critical mass, the world will no longer need to be shown a better way. And when we no longer need an example of individuals already aligned with their higher selves, the condition we know as autism will be no longer. The inexplicable capabilities of these children show us how our modern view of the physical world is extremely limited, but when we consider the big picture of who they are in their totality, we will begin to see how all the pieces fall into place rather brilliantly. These children have come with intent. They have emerged in the numbers that they have to share an idea.

With this idea we can choose to look at a child with autism not as the victim of a terrible tragedy but as a messenger of love.

It's been clear to us for a long time that Jack likes math. He seems to embrace the concrete, symmetrical quality of mathematical problem solving, and because of this we started introducing triangles and other explorations of geometry in the playroom. We brought a few work sheets in and he really got excited when he saw one in particular—one that featured a polyhedron.

Polyhedrons are three-dimensional geometric shapes that have concrete properties. After he was introduced to the polyhedrons, we googled them and compiled images of them onto printouts. We spent many, many hours with Jack constructing them out of origami, wooden dowels, straws, clay, and even playing cards. He would talk about them, stare at them, and build them out of any building sets he had like Lego, K'Nex, or magnetic tiles. We made books out of images of them and he took these various samples to bed with him. This interest of his also became an outlet through which he learned to better empathize with others when he decided to make origami polyhedrons into gifts for his teachers.

About the time I began writing this book, Jack entered a phase in which he perseverated on a certain image of a tetrahedron. A tetrahedron is one of the platonic solids, or polyhedrons in which every face of the shape is a polygon and each intersection of the shape is composed of the same number of faces. This is also true of cubes, which have six faces, as well as three other shapes. A tetrahedron has four polygonal faces, all of which are triangles.

About halfway through my writing this book, my family and I all went out to Big Sur, California, for a brief holiday. Before we left, Jack presented me with an image of the tetrahedron and asked me to take a picture of it so I could print out a larger version. I did this with my phone.

While we were in Big Sur, we visited our favorite restaurant. The restaurant has a gift shop attached to it, and because I had just worked on the chapter about shamanism and the ecstasy of death, I found myself attracted to a book called *Shamanic Awakening.* This book was written by a woman who explored her journey through shamanism and working with the living energies of the world. On our flight home I read about how, beyond war zones and places like Chernobyl, the darkest energy exists in places like prisons and hospitals.

But she explored the lighter side of energy as well. In the book, she states that everyone on earth has a *Merkaba,* which is an energy field of living light that surrounds them. By practicing certain breathing techniques and visualizations, we can access this energy field and use it as a vehicle to express the light we have within ourselves. Doing so will elevate us to higher dimensions of consciousness.

The Merkaba exists as a geometric shape. The form it takes is a tetrahedron, which was depicted on the page as an image.

It was the very same configuration of a tetrahedron that was on my phone, that Jack had perseverated on for months.

I see where humanity is lacking. So many of us choose to suffer, to accept that love can be felt and expressed only under certain conditions. But when I sat there looking at the image in that book, I was reminded of that which I had been slowly discovering every day that I was fortunate enough to be a parent of a child diagnosed with autism.

Each of us has the potential to live in a higher frequency of life. Each of us can shed the beliefs that limit us in the favor of those that affirm us. Each of us is capable of unconditional love. Each of us can surround the world around us in a field of light.

AFTERWORD

I will never forget the intense emotions I felt when Jack was first diagnosed with autism. Nor do I believe you will ever forget those first few days with your own child. I am sure the feelings are etched into your heart as deeply as they are etched into mine. But they serve a purpose. They serve as a catalyst for change.

There is an enormous amount at stake here. The life of your child with autism lies in your very hands. It is your choice. You can choose fear or you can choose love. If you choose love, your child has a very real chance of finding his way to health, existing comfortably in this world, having meaningful relationships, and living a life that he was meant to live, a life of unlimited possibilities. And when you choose love, the transformation that will take place in your life as well as your child's will far surpass any previous expectation you may have had of having a "normal" life.

Society does a great job dictating what is normal. But I no longer want "normal" for myself or any of my children, least of all Jack—whose "atypical" way of being in this world has been a beckoning for me to understand and meet him where he is. By doing so, I have discovered the real meaning of being human. To be human is to live with compassion, acceptance, tolerance, joy, and love. My hope for you is that by intervening on your child's behalf and aligning yourself with the message he is here to share, you will continue to embody these qualities in yourself.

Each of us has an amazing opportunity to evolve, should we choose to walk down that path with our very special children.

RESOURCES

The websites and products I have listed here are compiled to offer suggestions only. There are many resources available that provide expertise and guidance beyond the scope of this book. It is my intention for the below suggestions to help you continue educating yourself on what might be best for your child. For more of my favorites and ongoing recommendations related to healing and embracing autism and self, please visit my website at www.andrealibutti.com.

Therapies to Explore

Acupuncture

Nambudripad's Allergy Elimination Techniques: www.naet.com

Homeopathy

CEASE Therapy: www.cease-therapy.com
Complete Elimination of Autistic Spectrum Expression (CEASE) therapy

Sequential Homeopathy: www.heilkunst.com
Hahnemann Center for Heilkunst in Ottawa, Canada. (They do phone consults so you don't have to travel to Canada.)

Homotoxicology

Mary Coyle in New York City:
www.realchildcenter.com

Hyperbaric oxygen therapy

OxyHealth:
www.oxyhealth.com

Neurofeedback

The Othmer Method:
www.brianothmerfoundation.org for information
www.eeginfo.com for a list of practitioners

Son-Rise Program®

The Autism Treatment Center of America™:
www.autismtreatmentcenter.org

Home and Personal-Care Resources

Building biologists

Check the electromagnetic radiation levels in your home and learn more at the Healthy Building Environment Learning Center:
www.hbelc.org

Personal-care products

Learn about the safety of various products at the Environmental Working Group's "Skin Deep" database:
www.ewg.org

Water filters

Aquasana:
www.aquasana.com

Dietary Resources

Comprehensive website addressing dietary issues

Julie Matthews, Certified Nutrition Consultant:
www.nourishinghope.com

For gastrointestinal healing

Specific Carbohydrate Diet (SCD):
www.breakingtheviciouscycle.info

For severe digestive issues

Feingold Diet:
www.feingold.org

Recommended Supplements

Great online resource for most supplements

Emerson Ecologics:
www.emersonecologics.com

Chlorella

Sun Chlorella offers a whole form of this superfood:
www.sunchlorellausa.com

Digestive enzymes

Enzymedica brand:
www.enzymedica.com

Lomatium dissectum

LDM-100 is my must-have for colds and flus:
www.barlowherbal.com

Multivitamin and multiminerals

BrainChild Nutritionals designs supplements specifically for autism, ADHD, and environmental health concerns: www.brainchildnutritionals.com

Omega-3 Supplement

"Speak" by Nourish Life and Speech Nutrients: www.speechnutrients.com

Phosphatidylcholine (PC)

I recommend BodyBioPC for cell membrane health: www.bodybio.com

Probiotics

Klaire Labs brand offers many beneficial combos: www.klaire.com

Theralac by Master Supplements: www.theralac.com

Recommended Books Written by Persons with Autism

Grandin, Temple. *Thinking in Pictures*

Higashida, Naoki. *The Reason I Jump: The Inner Voice of a Thirteen-Year-Old Boy with Autism*

Kaufman, Raun. *Autism Breakthrough: The Groundbreaking Method that Has Helped Families All over the World*

Mukhopadhyay, Tito Rajarshi. *How Can I Talk If My Lips Don't Move?: Inside My Autistic Mind*

Stillman, William. *Autism and the God Connection*

Tammet, Daniel. *Born on a Blue Day: Inside the Extraordinary Mind of an Autistic Savant*

Williams, Donna. *Autism and Sensing: The Unlost Instinct*

Favorite Books That Have Helped Me on My Journey

Alexander, Eben. *Proof of Heaven: A Neurosurgeon's Journey into the Afterlife*

Beck, Martha. *Expecting Adam: A True Story of Birth, Rebirth, and Everyday Magic*

Chopra, Deepak. *Quantum Healing: Exploring the Frontiers of Mind/Body Medicine*

Dass, Ram. *Be Here Now*

Dyer, Wayne. *Wishes Fulfilled: Mastering the Art of Manifesting*

Foundation for Inner Peace. *A Course in Miracles*

Grout, Pam. *E-Squared: Nine Do-It-Yourself Energy Experiments that Prove Your Thoughts Create Your Reality*

Hawkins, David R. *Transcending the Levels of Consciousness: The Stairway to Enlightenment*

Hay, Louise. *You Can Heal Your Life*

Hicks, Esther and Jerry. *Ask and It Is Given: Learning to Manifest Your Desires*

Kaufman, Barry Neil. *Son-Rise: The Miracle Continues*

Lipton, Bruce. *The Biology of Belief: Unleashing the Power of Consciousness, Matter, and Miracles*

McCandless, Jaquelyn. *Children with Starving Brains: A Medical Treatment Guide for Autism Spectrum Disorder*

Moorjani, Anita. *Dying to Be Me: My Journey from Cancer, to Near Death, to True Healing*

Nepo, Mark. *The Book of Awakening: Having the Life You Want by Being Present to the Life You Have*

Ramtha. *The White Book*

Tolle, Eckhart. *A New Earth: Awakening to Your Life's Purpose*

Walsch, Neale Donald. The *Conversations with God* series

Weiss, Brian. *Many Lives, Many Masters: The True Story of a Prominent Psychiatrist, His Young Patient, and the Past-Life Therapy that Changed Both Their Lives*

❊ ❊ ❊

REFERENCES

Introduction

Mukhopadhyay, Tito Rajarshi. *How Can I Talk If My Lips Don't Move?: Inside My Autistic Mind.* New York: Arcade Publishing, 2008.

Chapter 1

FDA. "FDA Proposes New Warnings About Suicidal Thinking, Behavior in Young Adults Who Take Antidepressant Medications." Retrieved from www.fda.gov /NewsEvents/Newsroom/PressAnnouncements/2007/ucm108905.htm.

Markram, Henry, Tania Rinaldi, and Kamila Markram. "The Intense World Syndrome: An Alternative Hypothesis for Autism." *Frontiers in Neuroscience* 1, no. 1 (2007): 77–96, doi: 10.3389/neuro.01/1.1.006.2007.

Chapter 2

Adams, JB, F George, and T Audhya. "Abnormally High Plasma Levels of Vitamin B6 in Children with Autism Not Taking Supplements Compared to Controls Not Taking Supplements." *Journal of Alternative and Complementary Medicine* 12, no. 1 (2006): 59–63.

American Psychiatric Association. *Diagnostic and Statistical Manual of Mental Disorsders;* fifth edition. Arlington, VA: American Psychiatric Publishing, 2013.

Goines, Paula, and Judy Van de Water. "The Immune System's Role in the Biology of Autism." *Current Opinion in Neurology* 23, no. 2 (2011): 111–17, doi: 10.1097/ WCO.0b013e3283373514.

Goldani, Andre, et al. "Biomarkers in Autism." *Frontiers in Psychiatry* 5 (2014): 100, doi: 10.3389/fpsyt.2014.00100.

McDougle, Christopher, and William Carlezon Jr.. "Neuroinflammation and Autism: Toward Mechanisms and Treatments." *Neuropsychopharmacology Reviews* 38 (2013): 241–42, doi: 10.1038/npp.2012.174.

Chapter 3

Autism and Developmental Disabilities Monitoring Network. "Community Report on Autism 2014." *CDC*. Retrieved from www.cdc.gov/ncbddd/autism/states/comm_report_autism_2014.pdf.

California Department of Public Health. "First Drinking Water Standard for Hexavalent Chromium Now Final." June 3, 2014. Retrieved from www.cdph.ca.gov/Pages/NR14-053.aspx.

Dean, Amy, and Jennifer Armstrong. "Genetically Modified Foods." *American Academy of Environmental Medicine*. Retrieved from www.aaemonline.org/gmopost.html.

Environmental Protection Agency. "An Introduction to Indoor Air Quality (IAQ)." Page last updated July 9, 2012. Retrieved from www.epa.gov/iaq/voc.html.

Environmental Working Group. "Body Burden: The Pollution in Newborns." July 14, 2005. Retrieved from www.ewg.org/research/body-burden-pollution-newborns.

Environmental Working Group. "State 'Clean Up' Plan Could Leave 24 Million Californians Exposed to Potent Carcinogen." October 11, 2013. Retrieved from www.ewg.org/release/state-clean-plan-could-leave-24-million-californians-exposed-potent-carcinogen.

Palmer, RF, S Blanchard, and R Wood. "Proximity to Point Sources of Environmental Mercury Release as a Predictor of Autism Prevalence." *Health & Place* 15, no. 1 (2009): 18–24, doi: 10.1016/j.healthplace.2008.02.001.

Roberts, AL, et al. "Perinatal Air Pollutant Exposures and Autism Spectrum Disorder in the Children of Nurses' Health Study II Participants." *Environmental Health Perspectives* 121, no. 8 (2013): 978–84, doi: 10.1289/ehp.1206187.

Roberts, EM, et al. "Maternal Residence Near Agricultural Pesticide Applications and Autism Spectrum Disorders Among Children in the California Central Valley." *Environmental Health Perspectives* 115, no. 10 (2007): 1482–89, doi: 10.1289/ehp.10168.

World Health Organization. "Children's Environmental Health: Air Pollution." Retrieved from www.who.int/ceh/risks/cehair/en.

Chapter 4

Barnes, Patricia, Barbara Bloom, and Richard Nahin. "Complementary and Alternative Medicine Use Among Adults and Children: United States, 2007." *National Health Statistic Reports.* December 10, 2008. Retrieved from www.cdc.gov/nchs /data/nhsr/nhsr012.pdf.

Belon, P, et al. "Histamine Dilutions Modulate Basophil Activation." *Inflammation Research* May 53, no. 5 (2004): 181–88.

De Vernejoul, P, et al. "Isotopic Approach to the Visualization of Acupuncture Meridians." *Agressologie* 25, no. 10 (1984): 1107–11.

Ennis, Madeleine. "Basophil Models of Homeopathy: A Sceptical View." *Homeopathy* 99, no. 1 (2010): 51–56, doi: 10.1016/j.homp.2009.11.005.

Vickers, Andrew, et al. "Acupuncture for Chronic Pain: Individual Patient Data Meta-analysis." *Archives of Internal Medicine* 172, no. 19 (2012): 1444–53, doi: 10.1001/archinternmed.2012.3654.

Chapter 5

American Psychiatric Association. *Diagnostic and Statistical Manual of Mental Disorders,* fifth edition. Arlington, VA: American Psychiatric Publishing, 2013.

Grandin, Temple. *Thinking in Pictures: My Life with Autism.* New York: Random House, 1995.

Higashida, Naoki. *The Reason I Jump.* New York: Random House, 2013.

Mukhopadhyay, Tito Rajarshi. *How Can I Talk If My Lips Don't Move?: Inside My Autistic Mind.* New York: Arcade Publishing, 2008.

Mukhopadhyay, Tito Rajarshi. *The Mind Tree: A Miraculous Child Breaks the Silence of Autism.* New York: Arcade Publishing, 2000.

Chapter 6

Alexander, Eben. *Proof of Heaven: A Neurosurgeon's Journey into the Afterlife.* New York: Simon and Schuster, 2012.

CDC. "Autism and Developmental Disabilities Monitoring (ADDM) Network." Last updated April 9, 2014. Retrieved from www.cdc.gov/ncbddd/autism /addm.html.

Isaacson, Rupert. *The Horse Boy: A Memoir of Healing.* New York: Little, Brown and Company, 2009.

YJ Editor. "New Study Finds 20 Million Yogis in U.S." *Yoga Journal.* December 5, 2012. Retrieved from www.yogajournal.com/uncategorized/new-study-finds-20-million-yogis-u-s.

Chapter 7

Gallup. "State of the American Workplace." Retrieved from www.gallup.com /services/178514/state-american-workplace.aspx.

Jones, Sparrow Rose. "ABA." *Unstrange Mind.* October 7, 2014. Retrieved from https://unstrangemind.wordpress.com/2014/10/07/aba.

US Department of Health and Human Services. "Mental Health: A Report of the Surgeon General." Rockville, MD: U.S. Department of Health and Human Services, Substance Abuse and Mental Health Services Administration, Center for Mental Health Services, National Institutes of Health, National Institute of Mental Health, 1999. Retrieved from http://profiles.nlm.nih.gov/ps/access/NNBBHS.pdf.

Chapter 8

The Autism Treatment Center of America. Retrieved from www.autismtreatment center.org.

Higashida, Naoki. *The Reason I Jump.* New York: Random House, 2013.

Chapter 10

Corcoran, Sandra. *Shamanic Awakening: My Journey Between the Dark and the Daylight.* Rochester, VT: Bear and Company, 2014.

Hawkins, David. *Power vs. Force: The Hidden Determinants of Human Behavior,* revised edition. Carlsbad, CA: Hay House, 2014.

Hicks, Esther and Jerry. *Ask and It Is Given: Learning to Manifest Your Desires.* Carlsbad, CA: Hay House, 2004.

Watson, Lyall. *Lifetide: A Biology of the Unconscious.* New Rochelle, NY: Scepter Publishing, 1987.

ACKNOWLEDGMENTS

I am so grateful to Louise Hay for being who she is and creating Hay House, a place where many authors have inspired me in my journey. Thank you, Reid Tracy, for granting me this opportunity to share my message with the world. Thank you, Alex Freemon and Nicolette Salamanca Young, for having enough faith to believe I could take the manuscript from its original form to what it is today. Thank you, Neil Gordon, my writing coach, who held my hand through the entire process, and whose brilliance and expertise guided me with such kindness; I never could have done it without you.

Thank you to Bears and Samahria Kaufman, whose vision has lit up thousands of lives and whose guidance taught me how to approach my son from a place of acceptance and compassion. And to Raun Kaufman for being the amazing human being that you are today. I have so much appreciation for all of the people at the Autism Treatment Center of America and the Option Institute for showing us all a better way.

I am immensely grateful to the teachers who work with my son, inspiring him to want to connect from a place deep inside himself. Janel Duffy, Ashley Millerd, Elizabeth Smith, Erin Skaalerud, David Mannes, Jennifer Cucinotta, and Jennifer Folbert, thank you for your unending energy, excitement, and enthusiasm. Thank you, Jan Achilich, for believing in my far-out ideas and always supporting me.

A special thank you to Sidney Baker, who took me under his wing and mentored me. I appreciate all of your time and your big heart in helping my family and me over the years.

And to my husband, Pat, for letting me go where I needed to go, physically and spiritually, to heal myself and our family. Thank you for a love that no one else has ever shown me. Thank you, Jack, for inspiring all of this and putting up with all of us. Thank you, Sammy, for your big heart and your sweet soul; I'm in awe of you daily. And thank you to my little miracle boy, Ben, who inspires me daily to be a better person.

And finally, thank you to my spirit posse of love and light, for always leading me to my answer.

🧩 🧩 🧩

ABOUT THE AUTHOR

Andrea Libutti, M.D., is a board-certified emergency medicine physician and spent several years in private practice treating children with autism. She took significant steps to establish a viable process for addressing the needs of children with autism when her oldest son, Jack, was diagnosed at 20 months old.

She has come to understand the disorder from a mind-body-spirit perspective and feels the most beneficial approach to a child with autism embraces all of these aspects. She also sees the need for a paradigm shift surrounding the belief that the diagnosis of autism is a tragedy. Dr. Libutti believes that if we shift our beliefs about these children and allow ourselves to see the brilliance in who they are, the health and well-being of our families and perhaps even our world will improve beyond what we thought possible. You can find educational, informational, and inspirational topics related to responding to autism and healing the self on her website at www.andrealibutti.com.

Dr. Libutti received her medical training from the University of Southern California and conducted her residency at Beth Israel Medical Center in Manhattan. She lives on Long Island with her husband, their three sons, and their golden retriever named Abby.

We hope you enjoyed this Hay House book.
If you'd like to receive our online catalog featuring additional
information on Hay House books and products, or if you'd like to
find out more about the Hay Foundation, please contact:

Hay House, Inc., P.O. Box 5100, Carlsbad, CA 92018-5100
(760) 431-7695 or (800) 654-5126
(760) 431-6948 (fax) or (800) 650-5115 (fax)
www.hayhouse.com® • www.hayfoundation.org

Published and distributed in Australia by: Hay House Australia Pty. Ltd.,
18/36 Ralph St., Alexandria NSW 2015
Phone: 612-9669-4299 • *Fax:* 612-9669-4144 • www.hayhouse.com.au

Published and distributed in the United Kingdom by: Hay House UK, Ltd.,
Astley House, 33 Notting Hill Gate, London W11 3JQ
Phone: 44-20-3675-2450 • *Fax:* 44-20-3675-2451 • www.hayhouse.co.uk

Published and distributed in the Republic of South Africa by:
Hay House SA (Pty), Ltd., P.O. Box 990, Witkoppen 2068
Phone/Fax: 27-11-467-8904 • www.hayhouse.co.za

Published in India by: Hay House Publishers India,
Muskaan Complex, Plot No. 3, B-2, Vasant Kunj, New Delhi 110 070
Phone: 91-11-4176-1620 • *Fax:* 91-11-4176-1630 • www.hayhouse.co.in

Distributed in Canada by: Raincoast Books,
2440 Viking Way, Richmond, B.C. V6V 1N2
Phone: 1-800-663-5714 • *Fax:* 1-800-565-3770 • www.raincoast.com

Take Your Soul on a Vacation

Visit www.HealYourLife.com® to regroup, recharge,
and reconnect with your own magnificence.
Featuring blogs, mind-body-spirit news, and life-changing
wisdom from Louise Hay and friends.

Visit www.HealYourLife.com today!

31901056107396

CPSIA information can be obtained
at www.ICGtesting.com
Printed in the USA
FSOW01n1939170215
5220FS